THE ULTIMATE INVESTMENT

MARK B. MURPHY

THE
ULTIMATE
INVESTMENT

*A Roadmap to Grow Your Business
and Build Multigenerational Wealth*

Forbes | Books

Published by Forbes Books, Charleston, South Carolina.
Member of Advantage Media.

Forbes Books is a registered trademark, and the Forbes Books colophon is a trademark of Forbes Media, LLC.

Printed in the United States of America.

10 9 8 7 6 5 4 3 2 1

ISBN: 978-1-955884-25-9 (Hardcover)
ISBN: 978-1-955884-68-6 (eBook)

LCCN: 2022911540

Cover design by Matthew Morse.
Layout design by Amanda Haskin.

This custom publication is intended to provide accurate information and the opinions of the author in regard to the subject matter covered. It is sold with the understanding that the publisher, Forbes Books, is not engaged in rendering legal, financial, or professional services of any kind. If legal advice or other expert assistance is required, the reader is advised to seek the services of a competent professional.

Since 1917, Forbes has remained steadfast in its mission to serve as the defining voice of entrepreneurial capitalism. Forbes Books, launched in 2016 through a partnership with Advantage Media, furthers that aim by helping business and thought leaders bring their stories, passion, and knowledge to the forefront in custom books. Opinions expressed by Forbes Books authors are their own. To be considered for publication, please visit **books.Forbes.com**.

(Cue the theme song from a popular 1970s sitcom ...)
To my Murphy-DeMayo bunch and all blended families …
Here's the story of a lovely lady
Who was bringing up three very lovely kids.
All of them had hair of brown like their mother,
The youngest one so cute.
Here's the story of a man named Murphy
Who was bringing up two boys of his own.
They were three men living all together,
Yet they were all alone.
Till the one day when the lady met this fellow,
And they knew it was much more than a hunch
That this group would somehow form a family.
That's the way we became the Murphy-DeMayo bunch.

Lisa DeMayo, my wife, my partner, my lover, my friend,
You make every day better for everyone, especially me.
You are the straw that stirs our family's drink.
I waited a long time to meet you!

Lucas, Gianna, Bennett, Victoria, and Nick, my children,
You are all hardworking, thoughtful, and respectful.
Let's continue to celebrate life every day!

CONTENTS

INTRODUCTION

〰

I'm in Las Vegas, giving a speech to several thousand dentists. The room is vast. I stand under the spotlight to address the crowd. I see them, but I also feel their penetrating gazes and keen ears, hanging on my every word. These are men and women from across the nation who have their own dentistry practices. They are accomplished, eager, ambitious.

I ask them a question, a seemingly simple one: "How many of you consider yourself to be entrepreneurs?" My voice echoes from the speakers situated strategically around the room and bounces off the walls. A sea of hands shoots up. I smile, and then I deliver the bombshell: despite what they think, I tell them, they are *not* entrepreneurs. Not in the truest sense, at least. I watch their befuddled and wary expressions process this statement. Then I spend the next few minutes explaining. The majority of them ran their own practices and owned their own "jobs," not their own businesses. Sure, they had a practice, a front-desk receptionist, even a dental assistant, but at the end of the day, unless they showed up to fill cavities and examine enamel, their offices could not and would not function, and the money wouldn't come in. They were trading time for money—just like in a job—instead of freeing up time so they could grow their businesses, accumulate exponential wealth, and leave a legacy for future generations. "You can't achieve freedom," I explained, "to work and live as you please because you're not able to overcome the constraints of time." If they were spending their days drilling teeth, when would they find time to achieve anything else? Then I proceeded to show them what their businesses, their bank balances, and their lives could look like if they truly did learn to shift from having a day job to being an entrepreneur in the truest sense. Many were taken aback, bemused, and more than a little surprised.

Unfortunately, this story isn't exclusive to just those thousands of people in that room. And not just to dentists either. For too many entrepreneurs hailing from all industries across the spectrum, owning a business becomes about working with such single-minded focus that they miss out on all the beauties of true entrepreneurship and the wonderful things it can yield them: more time, less dependency, more money, and a better quality of life for them and their families.

Entrepreneurs are naturally unconventional, outside-the-box thinkers. It's what makes them successful and so great at what they do. Because if they thought just like everybody else, they wouldn't be blazing new paths for themselves and making the world an easier or better place for others.

That brings us to me—and this book. Let's start with me. Who am I to be giving you this guidance? Why even listen to what I say? Well, for starters, I am a key business strategist, critical thinker, and financial advisor to entrepreneurs or entrepreneurial-thinking people. It sounds fancy, I know. To be honest I wasn't always experienced in all things money. Decades ago I graduated from the Kelley School of Business at Indiana University with a finance degree. And then I started the job hunt. Fortunately, a major insurance company offered me $1,000 a month, which was $1,000 more than I was making.

I always like to say the number one job of an entrepreneur is confidence—always believe in and bank on yourself. Based on this definition, I suppose I've been an entrepreneur from the get-go. I took the $1,000-a-month job, and I felt pretty good about it … until I read an article that said the average person graduating from business school that year was making $28,000. Back then that was a lot of money. When I read this, the first thing I did was lease a BMW, which was around a $300-a-month payment. Why? Because I was letting that entrepreneurial confidence lead my actions. I felt a BMW was what I imagined a successful person would own—a person making $28,000. I thought, hell, if the average person gets paid that much, I would do at least double that. So I made it a goal to earn at least $56,000 a year. With that and a few good suits, I set out as a financial advisor to make other people's lives better.

Today I can proudly say I've made a success of myself but, more importantly, of my clients.

For the last thirty-five years, I've coached entrepreneurial spirits to reach higher, go bigger than they imagined possible, and achieve their dreams. I've taught them to stop getting paid for what they do and start getting paid for what they know.

As of this book, I'm fifty-nine years old. I am fortunate enough to be able to easily retire this very moment if I wanted, and retire comfortably. So why am I still here? Writing this book? Running my firm? Because my job is my passion. It's my calling. Yours should be too. Many people work to retire, to get out of their job as soon as they can. But when you have a calling or a mission where you're transforming people's lives, and you wake up every day realizing you're making a difference, you won't want to retire.

This book is for any budding or aspiring or current entrepreneur. The field or industry you're in is irrelevant. The tips I share in this book can be applied by anyone at any level. Even if you're an employee clocking in at a nine-to-five, I'm confident this book will help you walk away with sound guidance. Whoever you are, whatever walk of life you come from, think of it as your road map to building multigenerational wealth.

In fact I wrote this book to document my thirty-six-year journey of coaching thousands of business owners into successful entrepreneurship. To talk about how I've helped them attain wealth for themselves and their future generations. After decades of helping, it struck me that the knowledge I share in this book is a necessity because so many clients I've worked with throughout the years have felt stuck in their business or careers at similar junctures. In working with me, they've transformed into entrepreneurs and investors. They've not only built multigenerational wealth, but they've also liberated their minds so they can enjoy, but also love, their lives and their businesses more than they imagined possible.

In this book I give you the same guidance I give to clients so you, too, can develop an entrepreneurial mindset and create a true business, reap financial benefits, and see your money and the quality of your life grow in positive directions.

What is an entrepreneurial mindset? An entrepreneurial mindset is uncommon or extraordinary thinking—it's thinking differently—asking the next big question. Because whoever asks the most powerful questions and thinks the deepest wins.

And that's exactly the purpose of this book: to teach you how to win, how to create a business that eliminates or reduces costs and competition. But that takes getting the organization to grow to where it's no longer centered around the entrepreneur's ability to produce a function or do the work.

A terrible truth is that most companies never get past the self-employed stage because they're still running their businesses like a start-up. A company that employs ten, twenty, fifty, one hundred, two hundred, etc. employees but still focuses on the talent of the entrepreneur cannot grow. In this book I'll teach you the difference between being self-employed and being a business owner who can grow wealth for themselves and their future generations.

What many fail to realize is that the roles of entrepreneur and business owner require different sets of skills. Most entrepreneurs don't go to school to learn how to hire and fire people or lead a group. And the skills that entrepreneurs are attracted to often aren't the same as those needed from the perspective of a business owner. As a result many never graduate beyond creating a job for themselves. But in shifting your mindset, suddenly, it's not so much about putting in the hours. It's about creating an organization that allows you to go from self-employed to business owner and then eventually to becoming an investor in that business. That is, if you want to.

But how can you get there? In this book I'll help you think entrepreneurially and therefore think bigger. I will show you that what you thought was impossible is not only possible, but it's also inevitable. I'll teach you the entrepreneurial mindset so that you can find your calling and live the life you want—and who retires from that?

WHEN YOU'VE BOUGHT YOURSELF A JOB INSTEAD OF A BUSINESS

Two decades ago I had a realization that forever transformed the way I viewed business. My dear friend and CEO of Fortune Management, Bernie Stoltz, and I were working with dentists from around the country. I noticed they were a cookie-cutter type in some ways. They all drove nice cars. They all sent their kids to great schools. They all took high-end vacations at exotic and luxurious places around the world. They were living the dream, enjoying life, and basking in the glow of success. But almost none of them were creating wealth, let alone generational wealth. Meaning none of their businesses were working to make money for them, or for their families, in the long run.

It became radically clear to me that people who didn't have an entrepreneurial mindset (as we defined in the intro), whether they were an employee or self-employed, were just drawing paychecks every few weeks. And once they had that paycheck in hand, paid taxes, scheduled bills and the mortgage, and paid for grocery and restaurant runs, perhaps squeezing a few dollars into their 401(k) or investment account, they'd be left with the bare minimum. At that pace, forty years later, they could almost indefinitely toss any notion of a comfortable retirement out the window.

Was this a guess or an exaggeration? I wish it were, but no, unfortunately, it is not. Many "successful" dentists take a step down in their retirement years—and not by choice. After decades of hard work running their own "businesses," they're forced to downsize from large, lavish homes to smaller ones, from two cars to one, and from the fanciest restaurants to the five-o'clock special. No doubt, it was not the life they imagined living after decades of hard work.

Unfortunately, it is only at that stage that realization dawns: all these decades, they had achieved little more than a temporarily comfortable life. Here I want to pause and say that for many people, that might be just fine and exactly what they're looking for. I'm not here to repudiate their thoughts or ambitions. But when someone hires me and my firm, my thought is that they didn't hire us just so they can live a temporarily comfortable life. They hired us to have a permanently *extraordinary* life. And that's exactly what we aim and plan to deliver.

We want to take you from drawing a paycheck and exchanging time for money (which is just like buying yourself a job!) to having an entrepreneurial mindset so you can set yourself up for an extraordinary life. Because the truth is a paycheck is simply a bribe to forget your dreams. To *achieve* your dreams, you have to think like an entrepreneur with an investor mindset. So let's hit on the investor part really quick because that's a key piece of the puzzle.

MOVING INTO THE INVESTOR CLASS

I was twenty-three years old when I launched my business. I financed the entire thing on my Visa credit card to the tune of about $20,000. That may be a considerable sum today, but back then it was a terrifying amount of money. I kept my living expenses spare and tried to reinvest as much of it as I could back in myself or the business. (In my world there are two types of transactions: expenses or investments, but more about that a little later.)

When I kicked off my own firm, I thought I had to do everything on my own, especially sales. This meant that for decades, I wound up working seventy-to-seventy-five-hour weeks. Sure, I had a very successful business, but had there been any disruption in my ability to perform, the whole thing would have come crashing down around me. Like the majority of our clients working in construction, hedge funds, private equity firms, medical professions, and other entrepreneurs, I wasn't really a business owner. Rather, I was self-employed. I'd bought myself a job, not a business, because the company couldn't survive without me.

Only when I used our transformational language to get a predictable result each time and then repeated the process over and over did I become a business owner. That language differentiated us from every other firm, and it became part of the culture of our company.

So what is transformational language exactly? It's language that transforms your relationship with clients. We could also call these memorable comments—or comments that stick in clients' minds. As a company we've created a list of things to say on a regular basis that our advisors use to get predictable results. And then we rinse and repeat, rinse and repeat.

The other thing to remember is that people almost never remember what you say; they remember how you make them feel. So also ask yourself: how do I make clients feel?

Today one of our main focuses is to help people go from being self-employed to becoming a business owner (who uses transformational language) and then to being an investor. How is this possible? Because when you transition from being self-employed to making it so that your company can operate in your absence, you're officially running a true business. And when that happens, it frees up time for you to then become an investor and have your money make money for you.

If you're an employee, I'm not suggesting you quit to become a business owner. Continue working, but you, too, should strive to become an investor. We aim to get our clients to invest in something that provides income regardless of whether or not they decide to work. But by investing, I don't just mean sticking money in your retirement fund.

If you asked Bill Gates how he became so successful, chances are he wouldn't say he's worth $130 billion because of his 401(k). He spent years and years avidly doing what I often coach my clients to do: he invested in his business, in real estate, and in financing deals.

But what's the most important investment of all, you might ask? What should take priority? I always tell clients that if they had only $1 to invest, the best investment someone with an entrepreneurial mindset would make is an investment in themselves (but more on that in a bit).

For now I would say before putting that money in an investment vehicle or using it to pay down a loan, consider putting it toward your business because that is what can generate an exponential rate of return compared with your other options. Think about it: your business can potentially double your income, but an investment vehicle like the stock market rarely has the rate of return to be able to do the same.

I know this guidance might come as a surprise to some because it's different or antithetical to what you hear from some financial and tax advisors, CPAs, attorneys, and other consultants. Usually, they'll advise you to invest in a fund or an insurance policy or a high-interest checking account. But as an experienced financial professional, I can tell you that that's not typically how you would succeed in building multigenerational wealth. It's how you would succeed in creating a comfortable lifestyle.

What's so terrible about comfort, you might ask? Comfort is a good thing, right? I don't disagree. But one thing you should also know and consider is that when you go for a comfortable lifestyle, you often become like a hamster in a wheel, running in circles faster and faster to keep up with your increasingly expensive tastes—and getting nowhere. You'll no longer be driving a Toyota Camry; now you'll be cruising in a Mercedes-Benz. You'll stop playing golf at the public course and instead join a fancy club. You'll have the ability to move to the better part of town with access to the best schools and, therefore, (also) higher taxes and higher costs. You

One of the keys to moving into the investor class is to defer this temptation of immediate gratification.

have more money, but at the same time, you're also spending more of it to afford your new, high-end luxurious life.

One of the keys to moving into the investor class is to defer this temptation of immediate gratification. Instead of building a lifestyle, feed the beast—your cash machine, also known as your business. This will provide you cash flow and asset value. It will help you build wealth with the value of the business. But if you fall into the trap of feeding your lifestyle first, you miss out on feeding the beast, meaning there'll be too much pressure on the cash flow. You won't be able to make good long-term decisions on the business end. You'll end up starving your business because the blood life of a business is cash—and not just to invest in your business but so that you're able to let that business grow in the best way possible with ample financial resources as needed versus being strapped and penny-pinching.

Then there are the effects of divorce or "the unexpected." Here's the truth, no matter how much we love to deny it: life happens. And it could happen to any one of us in any number of ways. For instance, according to many statistics, about 50 percent of the people in this country get divorced the first time, and 65 percent end up in divorce the second time.[1]

I see people coming into some success in their businesses. They adopt this lavish lifestyle instead of feeding the beast or their cash machine. And then life happens. They get divorced, for example, but the problem by then is that they've already established this lavish lifestyle. They're living in the big house. They're driving the fancy cars. They're at the fancy clubs. They're drinking imported beer, not domestic. They're taking fancy vacations, flying first class or private. And then suddenly with divorce, their cash flow and assets get cut in half. Now they begin to more resemble a person who's just starting out than someone who's been established in the business a while.

Unfortunately, it's not just divorce that could totally screw you over. It could be a lawsuit, an illness, an injury. It could be death. It

---

1   "How Common Is Divorce and What Are the Reasons?" YourDivorceQuestions.org, accessed June 2022, https://yourdivorcequestions.org/how-common-is-divorce/.

could be that your spouse has partners in a business and one of them dies or your spouse has a disagreement with their business partners and suddenly your money machine is messed up. Unfortunately, we all fall into the trap of believing that these misfortunes are never destined for us. We believe we would never experience any interruptions to cash flow. That we'll never get divorced. We'll never die. We'll never become disabled or get sued. That we'll never have a disagreement with that business partner or lose a key employer or key account.

But when it happens, we find ourselves trapped in a life without the ability to build wealth. We're just grinding it out for a paycheck, whether we're an employee or self-employed. That's why so few people have any true financial independence.

You don't want to be the hamster running in a wheel. You want money running after *you*. To be honest I didn't always know or think of it this way. The light bulb didn't turn on for me until I realized what was missing in my clients' lives—business owners from all across the country. As the ambition to help them build multigenerational wealth materialized in me, I realized I was a bit of a hypocrite because while I was coaching and guiding them to build wealth, I wasn't doing it for myself.

So how do we do that? How do we build wealth and multigenerational wealth? I talked about transformational language, which is part of the answer. But there's more to understanding how to be an investor—and a good one.

THE SECRETS OF INVESTORS

True business owners and investors understand the power of economies and the efficiencies of scale. They understand the power of replication and recurring revenue, but the self-employed and employees generally do not. It's about putting your efforts into the best opportunities.

For instance, too many businesses focus on just the top line rather than the bottom. It doesn't matter how much money or how much revenue you have. It's how much you get to keep and how much you earn. It's about the net profitability of the business, true, but then also the net profitability after taxes.

So what you'll see the ultrasharp operators try to do is drive as much revenue as they can through the same fixed overhead. If you have a dollar of revenue and you have the same fixed overhead and after you have paid all your expenses and all your fixed overhead, then what's left would be your profit. What I realized with economies and efficiencies of scale that I also have shared with my clients over the years is if you add a second dollar of revenue with the same fixed overhead and just incur some additional variable expenses for that dollar, you don't make double. Depending on the business, you can make quadruple or quintuple the amount you used to.

Presenting it slightly differently, if you have $1 million of recurring revenue, it is like having $20 million in the bank, earning 5 percent.

Now that we've established that, let's go back to the earlier example with the dentists to talk about some of the best secrets to becoming successful investors. These dentists' businesses revolved around their fine motor skills. If they couldn't work, their businesses would shut down. So I advised them to stop being "wet finger" dentists, making their earnings by working in people's mouths. I advised that they should hire other dentists and open more offices. If they had the ability to generate enough business for one doctor, why couldn't they generate enough for two doctors or for a second office?

They could use the right processes, strategies, transformational techniques, tools, and transformational language to replicate their original office. They would no longer be subject only to the whims of how well one doctor performed. Instead, they would develop core values, a core focus, and core principles uniformly across all their practices to create a business that was worth much, much greater than the sum of just one doctor.

I use dentists as an example, but this notion of expansion and replication is transferrable to almost any industry. For instance, when you go into a McDonald's—any McDonald's—you are handed a container of french fries that looks the same and tastes pretty much the same at any location across the nation. The employees are different, the layout of the store is more similar than different, the location is certainly different, but the experience and the food are pretty much the same. That's because this franchise has created a replicable process that delivers consistency across the board. It's not like if I buy a McDonald's franchise, I'll have to wonder, gee, how do I make french fries? Let me figure it out.

Nearly every business is replicable. Arguably, the only place where replication isn't possible is with our professional athlete and entertainer clients. An NFL quarterback can't subcontract work, and a rock star can't get a local church choir member to sing on stage for sixty thousand people. But that doesn't mean those people are out of luck. We have strategies for their money, too, so that they can buy into other businesses and companies. It just differs a bit from what I'm suggesting for everyone else. However, although the journey might be a bit different for these people, the destination is still the same: building wealth.

For the self-employed, the best secret to success requires getting over the founder's curse, where everything has to be perfect. You want your office to be clean, so you scrub it down. You want your books to be immaculate, so you do the accounting. You want to hire the best staff, so you do the recruiting. You want to attract as many clients as possible, so you do the marketing. You want your staff to be the best trained, so you do the onboarding and training. In the beginning it's you, you, you doing it all. This becomes a 24/7 drain on your time because you're confident only you can do almost all of the tasks better than someone who doesn't have a direct stake in your business. But there comes a time when you, as the founder, have to yield to the advice of Gino Wickman, author of *Traction: Get a Grip on Your Business*, and let go of the vine and leap. This means you learn to take a step back and trust in teamwork, as the saying goes. Be a leader and do what leaders do best: delegate. This isn't easy, but it is necessary. It requires patience and trust in the process so that you can ultimately have a business where you get paid for what you know, not what you do.

Now that we've uncovered some of the secrets to being an investor, let's uncover the basics of what it takes to build wealth.

CORE VALUES FOR BUILDING WEALTH

Many of us have been trained by the media and financial, tax, and legal professionals to focus on turning our money over to a money manager and then washing our hands clean, thinking our job is over and we'll no longer have another worry. I do believe every entrepreneur should have a good accountant, lawyer, and financial advisor. But too often, professionals in these industries fail to focus on some of the core values of multigenerational wealth building by overlooking these general principles:

1. Whoever asks the most powerful questions always wins. We have long said that the good ones tell and the great ones

ask—and this is true in business, too, particularly when you're in the profession of consulting or advising people. But many people, especially salespeople, make the mistake of telling when they should be asking. When you tell someone something, they can nod or disagree. But when you ask questions, it leads to collaboration. It also leads to a solution-focused effort to benefit you and your specific situation versus a cookie-cutter or assumed approach that could be a waste of time and benefit no one. Where the lawyers, attorneys, and financial advisors often fail is that speaking with clients should be somewhat of a discovery process. When you're speaking with clients, light bulbs should be going off in your brain where you start to see things clearer and clearer for the client as they share about themselves. That's what creates transformational or "aha" moments that can lead you to offering them the best advice or solution. And that can only be achieved by discovering your client through the right questions, not by talking at them or telling them things. There's also a more latent point here that's worth mention-ing in hopes I avoid you some heartache. Hire people who know how to stay in their "lanes." You can't have a lawyer giving financial advice, an accountant giving legal advice, or a financial advisor giving accounting advice. These consul-tants might feel they are trying to add value in some way by venturing beyond the boundaries of their "job lanes," but the truth is they are so far out of their league to even offer you advice they're clearly not the experts in. So part of your job as you're seeking the right professionals is making sure that you're surrounding yourself not only with the very best people in all areas and that you have not only the best team and best employers but also that you're creating a power team around you.

2. Go for the win-win outcome. Never get into a transaction where, for one party to win, the other must lose. Many professionals in this world think that life is a zero-sum game where only one person can win. They operate as though there's only a finite number of customers and possibilities out there. The win-win opportunity is to figure out a way where we are not cannibalizing each other, where we create abundance rather than scarcity, and where we create more so that everybody walks away better, and everybody wins.

3. We need to get out of the mindset of "I need that client— that's the only client in the world." We need to stop thinking that we have to beat somebody down to win. To create a win-win outcome, start by determining what's in the best interest of all parties and then the next step toward achieving that. Sometimes you may have to let a client go because you're not the right fit for them and vice versa—but in my books, that's a win for everyone involved, including the competitor who ends up taking them on.

4. Show up and be consistent. Kobe Bryant said he didn't understand lazy people, adding, "Great things come from hard work and perseverance." It's one thing to show up and another to be consistently good. This is the difference between good companies and great companies. A bad company is reactive. A great company is proactive. Also, the great companies show up consistently, not in spurts. There could be days when I am at the office, and I don't want to be there, or I'm having a bad day. But when a client shows

up, I have got to make sure that the hour or two hours I have with them is utter magic. Because consistency is key. When clients walk through my doors, every one of them knows exactly what to expect every single time. There are no surprises. This level of consistency is what builds trust and confidence in clients. And that, in part, is what makes them want to stay loyal to you.

I've represented many athletes over the years, and I've noticed something important about how they train or, perhaps, how they *don't* train. They don't train to perform the super fancy triple reverse kinds of moves that they might use once a season. Instead, they focus on the fundamentals, the kinds of moves they'll need to use regularly to succeed. That's how they get better.

In the same way, I can help you focus on the fundamental tools, techniques, training, and skill sets you'll need to get to the next level, whether that's going from self-employed to a business owner or going from an employee in your current job to an even better one you have your sights set on. If you fall into the former category, I'll help you focus on how you can be better at your role to make your company an even better company. If you're an employee, I'll help you take some cash flow and invest it to create abundance in your retirement while you aim higher up the corporate ladder. Either situation is a good starting place, and either one can still lead you to phenomenal results when it comes to building wealth.

This is where I often get asked another question: where's the best place to put my money—which brings us to my next topic.

THE BEST INVESTMENT

I've told people that the best investment you can make is to invest in yourself. Yet if we tell you to invest in yourself, that means those dollars are spent on you and not me or my company. But at our firm, we don't view our clients as potential dollars and cents toward our pocketbooks. We study them holistically and take their successes to mean ours.

When I reflect on my accomplishments since I kicked off this firm, I don't think first about the money I've generated for myself and my family. The most rewarding part of what I do, and the thought that comes to my mind first, is the number of businesses and entrepreneurial doorways I've helped open for clients. How those doorways and opportunities have helped clients buy homes, put food on the table, help their own families thrive and grow. All because of this little idea I was hopeful enough to pursue many decades ago. I think about how me working at my desk, meeting with parents and grandparents has had a ripple effect. How it's helped them send their kids and grandkids to college because of what we created, how it's created time for them to spend with those kids and grandkids.

My epitaph, which I hope is written many years from now, shouldn't tout how much money I made or that I helped people make a lot of money. I want to be remembered for transforming people's lives. I want to be imprinted on their minds and their family's hearts as someone who helped them live a better, more enriched life with their loved ones and, in turn, inspired them to help others too.

Be well read and surround yourself with good, ambitious, intelligent people.

And for that reason, I go back to my earlier point because I've learned that it is truly the key to success for us all: invest in yourself. Be well read and surround yourself with good, ambitious, intelligent people. When I say be well read, I don't just mean that you should read the top twelve business or self-help books. I mean read everything under the sun—about everything. Reading a wide variety of books on a wide variety of subjects will help you become a well-rounded person. Then make sure you also spend your time with people who encourage you to aim higher, to invest in yourself, and to do great things. Humans are like plants: they thrive based on the environment they are sowed in. Give a plant sunlight and water and it will grow and thrive. In the same way, if you surround yourself with bright, ambitious, good people, it creates an environment where you'll soak up that energy from around you. The stakes and the ante just keep getting higher as you continue to grow and flourish so that ultimately, success is but a foregone conclusion.

You might have heard the saying, "There's no right way to do the wrong thing. So just keep doing the right thing." I did just that and managed to get people to take a chance on me when I was just a twenty-three-year-old kid.

And I did that by doing the only thing people who have no experience can do: I worked harder. I got to places on time. I said please and thank you. I did what I said I would do. And I approached every person with a visceral belief that they would leave in a vastly better position after having spoken with me.

Finally, I had enthusiasm, which is contagious and infectious. People want to work with ambitious, motivated people who have a passion for what they do. They want to work with people who uplift them. And then if somebody, occasionally, would say to me "Well, why would I work with you? You're twenty-three years old. I could

work with somebody with ten or twenty or thirty years of experience."
My response to them would be "What if the people you've been
working with for thirty or forty years are not on the cutting edge of
what's going on in the world? Why don't you allow me to give you a
second opinion?" And either one of three things will happen: You'll
realize I'm the right person for your firm. You'll find out that the guys
you've been working with are doing a really good job for you, and all
I've done is confirm that. Or maybe you could take some of my ideas
and bring them back to the people you're working with.

Just give me an opportunity to change your life for the better.

You can get people to take a chance on you too. All you have
to do is answer this question: what am I willing to do that I'm not
already doing to have what I don't already have?

And if you are not willing to go above and beyond, are simply
self-employed, and are content with continuing that way, know that
you're pretty much being sold a paycheck that's stopping you from
attaining your dreams. Do you have the fortitude to dream that you
can have a life where you have not only financial freedom but also
freedom of time? If you're a business owner, are you interested in
diversifying your life, your wealth, and your focus on things other than
your core business? Are you looking to keep learning and growing so
you can move into the investor class? Do you want to create a bigger,
better life for yourself? Do you want to create it for your spouse or
your children and your grandchildren?

It's time to invest in you and in your business. I'll show you the way.

HARD WORK ISN'T ABOUT HOURS PUT IN

For many the entrepreneurial mindset is about working as many hours as possible, pouring every effort, every ounce of blood, sweat, and tears into growing the business. But what people fail to realize is that hard work shouldn't be equated to how much time you spend on or in your business. It should be about how much of an investment you put in planning. You can't grow exponentially with a small team that's focused on the same things year after year. Rather, you need a plan with the right collaborators and the best mentors.

The entrepreneurial mindset is about inhabiting a role where you have the autonomy to affect the outcome of your job, your business, or your project. Yet I see too many entrepreneurs placing all of their efforts behind pulling long hours all the time, nearly every day, month after month. Most of the time, it's a labor of love. Clients will tell me, "I'd like to double my income." Automatically, they translate that to mean, "Well, then I guess I will need to double my hours at work."

But give it some thought for a moment. If you're already working ten to fifteen hours a day and there are only twenty-four in a day, there's no way you could commit more time from your day. Not unless you want to camp out in your office and prop your mattress in a corner so you're pretty much living and breathing work and only work. But even then you'd need sleep to survive, which means more hours simply is not possible in any case. But say even if you were a machine that never needed sleep, food, or social interaction, there aren't enough hours in the day to possibly double your current number of hours worked.

That's where we need to shift our mindset and ideologies. Because the strategies that make you a successful self-employed person aren't the same strategies you need to make you a successful business owner. It's no longer about the number of hours you put in. Being a business owner means running an organization that extends beyond you.

So how do you do that? How do you make that possible?

You do it by leveraging human capital, technology, and alliance partners who may or may not be on your payroll. You create virtual alliances where the clients instantly recognize that there is something special going on. These include accountants, attorneys, bankers, and other people who can help facilitate your business's growth and take the burden of responsibility from your shoulders solely. Relationships with other organizations are also another type of alliance that allow your firm to tap into another's expertise, knowledge, and work without keeping them on your payroll. It's all about leverage. This brings us to the next point, which is how to leverage yourself—and the people around you—to their optimum.

HIGHEST AND BEST USE

Growing from entrepreneur to business owner takes work and effort. If you want to make it happen, the first thing to focus on is reframing your idea of hard work by making sure everybody in your firm is working in their highest and best use. What does this mean? It means that everybody is working in their unique ability. It used to bother me when I'd have an employee who was making $250,000 a year standing for four hours at the copy machine or ordering supplies. That was not their highest or best use. Not that they weren't competent at ordering supplies or making copies, but they weren't making the best use of their abilities or skill sets performing those tasks. I try to hire and train people to do the stuff I used to do, even though I'm more than capable of doing them, so I can attain my best and highest use. And then I encourage the people I hire to follow in my footsteps by hiring others who are better suited to certain roles and tasks they're currently responsible for. So like me, they're hiring people so they, too, can work toward *their* best and highest use. It might sound complicated, but it's actually a very simple process in practice. Once you follow this process, you'll end up with an organization that's really working and firing on all cylinders. Because everyone is working to their unique ability.

Also, it's important that everyone at your firm shares the same core values and knows their role so that you can row in the same direction. If you believe the core value of your company is to provide the best service but your staff believes it is to make the most money, you're already sitting at a conflict, meaning you are much less likely to row toward any real success.

Start with you, the entrepreneur, and then tap the key opinion leaders in your firm, all the way to the person who sweeps your floors, to make sure everyone knows what they're responsible for and feels confident in pursuing your company's common goal. As Jim Collins, author of *Good to Great*, says, you've got to put the right people in the right seats. That's how you create synergy.

It's important to maintain the highest and best use even when you get very busy. The most successful business owners know they need to review their roles every now and then. These reviews might reveal that a role needs to be modified, another needs to be combined, or a third is no longer necessary. There might be staff that suited a specific role a decade ago, but perhaps there's someone better in the organization to take it over today. Also, you might find that you now have resources you previously didn't to hire someone for work you once did or invest in technology to help with the work.

Having a team is important, but don't fool yourself into thinking that you have to train people to work at your level. Let's say you have ten people operating at 85 percent capacity of what you would if you would have done everything yourself. Well, then your organization is still plenty strong!

To be clear, we're not putting a team and all these resources in place so you can simply fold your arms, nod your head at the wonderful work being done and go play golf, or take an afternoon nap. We're encouraging these strides so that you can reach a higher and better use of your resources to benefit the growth of the company. You should complete the highest and best use analysis for every single person and every single expense in the organization. You should be looking to verify that everyone is in alignment, and if they're not, it's time to put them on the chopping board—preferably by helping them transition to another role within your company or outside of it where their highest and best use can be achieved. Remember: think win-win. If people cannot win with you, help them win elsewhere.

Now let's talk about the highest and best use of financial resources. When it comes to financial moves or expenses, I find that most of the time, entrepreneurs make decisions based on how much money they have or don't have in the bank account, not on the rate of return they're receiving for the money that's sitting there. Don't get me wrong. In my organization, expenses are always on the chopping block too. But potential investments are always in line and at the ready if I discover an avenue through which I am able to get at least a four- or five-to-one return or better. For those of you who aren't math whizzes, that's saying that if you put $5,000 into something, you should look to see at least a $20,000 or $25,000 return. That should be the critical analysis of whether your money is being put to the highest and best use, not whether you're having a good year or you've got extra money in the checkbook or the accountant said you should spend some money at the end of the year to lower your tax burden.

Speaking of tax burdens—don't be fooled by the "tricks." This is a bit of a tangent but well worth sneaking in here. Anytime a client conjures ways to reduce their tax burden, I have my answer at the ready.

"How do you plan to use your money to lower taxes?" I ask them.

If they reply, "I'm looking for a deduction of $200,000," I smile and say, "I'll give you a $300,000 deduction." When they ask how, I say, "I'm going to charge you $300,000 for this phone call."

Only then does the dawning of realization strike their expressions, and they understand that they're not making sound decisions grounded in critical thinking or logic but simply on emotion or circumstance.

When should you focus on making sound investments? Always. Even when times are tough and it seems daunting to make any moves, such as during a recession, you should aim at making the best and the most investments during those times, not the least. As Baron

Rothschild, an eighteenth-century member of the Rothschild banking family, once said, the best time to buy is when there's blood on the streets. You should always have an investment in play and expenses on the chopping block. It's how you'll start to build a healthy volume of money.

Once you've got a business where you are no longer responsible for running the day-to-day full time and you've built the amount of wealth that most of our clients have, your company will most likely become an important part of the portfolio of companies and investments that you own. And you'll have partners to make decisions with you and for you so it's not all on your shoulders. Being able to create that dependency on others yet independency for yourself is one of the greatest perks of being an entrepreneur—and a key component to growing wealth. The more time you have, the more acutely you can start to focus on using it to grow your money.

COACHES, MENTORS, AND ADVISORS

Once you are attaining your highest and best use, your work is not yet over. One of the things I recommend to my clients is to have a coach—maybe even more than one coach—no matter what business they're in. But I don't mean people with the specific title of coach or mentor, etc. I use those terms loosely to say that you must have somebody who can add value to your life. One of the best skill sets for an entrepreneur is to be a great listener to a mentor or coach or someone who adds value to your life because that presents an opportunity for you to learn from them. Sometimes when I say this, people think of engaging with someone older and wiser, and that can be great, but it doesn't always have to be those people who you learn from. I sometimes learn as much from younger people because they have a fresher perspective on life and are on the cutting edge of thinking.

When I was younger, however, I used to like to surround myself with older folks because they were wiser and more experienced in the world. But the bottom line is that I've always had mentors from as far back as I can remember. That constant learning and expansion of my own mind is what's helped me grow not only as a person but also as an entrepreneur.

In fact, when I saw how much this learning was helping me, I very deliberately set out to create my own informal board of directors so I could bounce ideas off others. I also am a voracious reader, and I devour a wide variety of books—not just business and self-improvement books but also fiction and nonfiction. This allows me to expand my thinking and think differently so I can provide more value to clients. Because the more value I can create, the easier it is to get people to pay me.

At different points in my life, I remember being taken under the wings of some brilliant professionals. In my early thirties, for instance, I met Harris Rothstein, the managing partner and CEO of Rothstein Kass and Co., who let me shadow and observe how he ran his business. This man was fascinating and ran one of the most prolific accounting and consulting firms in the country. I enjoyed sitting with him and soaking up everything I possibly could from observing

One of the best skill sets for an entrepreneur is to be a great listener to a mentor or coach or someone who adds value to your life because that presents an opportunity for you to learn from them.

how he operated his business. Till this day, I look for people I respect in business or from my peer group to learn from and improve myself.

Apart from getting a great coach or advisor or mentor, another thing I advise entrepreneurs to do is to surround themselves with people whose conversations leave them elevated or stimulated in some way, either intellectually or personally. If you want to see what your life looks like in ten years, you don't need a magic ball or a fortune-teller. Just look at the books you read and the people you hang out with, professionally and personally—they are the best indication as to what your future will look like. I'm sure this probably isn't news to most of you. Many have heard the saying that you're the average of the five people you hang out with most. That doesn't mean you stop hanging out with old buddies or cut connections from decades-old friendships. That's not at all the implication here. Keep going out and drinking beers with your buddies behind your old high school on Saturday nights. But also know that you need another group of cronies to lift you up beyond just a personal level. Because guzzling beers with a bunch of friends isn't going to lift you or propel you in life. But setting time aside to meet with people who have immense drive and ambition will pump up your spirits, give you ideas for your own life, and take you to that next elevated level.

I don't just talk the talk here. I practice what I preach, and I've seen the results firsthand. For more than a quarter-century, I've been a part of a study group composed of some very sharp men; we are like brothers. You've heard of study groups in school where a group of people get together and study for an exam so they can ace the test. This "study group" operates much in the same way, except our goal is to ace in business and in life. We all have each other's back, and we operate like a small community that bolsters each other on a personal and professional level to do better, aim higher, and achieve more. We share ideas where we can and try to push one another to attain things that initially might seem impossible. But when you're part of such an abundant group, I've found that suddenly the impossible seems possible and the possible becomes probable.

This group, time and time again, has inspired and encouraged me to become the very best I can possibly be in my industry. I've also worked with mastermind groups of people from other industries and organizations, and I've sat on many boards of directors of private equity companies. These experiences have allowed me to see how other businesses operate while I immerse my mind in the company and ideations of an awful lot of smart people. When you surround yourself with sharp, forward-thinking people who possess an entrepreneurial mindset, you will grow, and so will your business. But there's more to growth than just coaches and mentors and advisors.

DISRUPTABLE THINKING

One of the keys to growth and longevity is being adaptable to change. Every business is dealing with disruption on a radical level at any given point. Look at the past several decades as evidence. In our lifetime we've lived through a great recession, a pandemic, and (in some cases) a few wars to boot. In the midst of these upheavals, businesses have had to adapt and change to the disruption, sometimes in drastic ways. Banks have shuttered branches in favor of online banking. The workforce has shifted from a healthy in-person setting to hybrid and completely remote roles. People have gone from relying on gas to growing skeptical of the unpredictable prices per barrel, tilting more in favor than ever toward hybrid or electric cars. All of these changes have affected businesses on multiple levels—and the successful businesses are the ones that have learned to adjust to the disruptions by overcoming hurdles while also finding a way to adapt better for the future.

The best way to continue your growth is to remain open to disruptable thinking so that your business isn't vulnerable. Look at any point in history and you will notice that disruption has often brought about change, which has resulted in growth for those willing to adapt—be it from war, strife, or anything else. In the same way, disrupting our thinking in new, challenging ways will do the same—it will help you grow and your business grow. True, successful entrepreneurs will never—and have never—do the same thing forever. They are constantly innovating, changing, and elevating their thoughts and their work to make sure that they are on the cutting edge of disruption. Sometimes they are the disruption itself.

One huge example of disruption is the internet, which has affected the marketplace by cutting out the middleman. Companies that had been around for 150 or 200 years disappeared within a year or two because of the internet and its disruption in the marketplace. Those who've been around long enough might remember Blockbuster, a brick-and-mortar movie store that rented videos and DVDs. A little red kiosk, called Red Box, often found in grocery stores, disrupted the market and gave Blockbuster a run for its money. Then came streaming services from the likes of Netflix, Disney+, and HBO Max. Rarely do you ever have to step out of the house now to cozy up to a good movie, unless you decide to make the occasional trek to a movie theater.

The best way to continue your growth is to remain open to disruptable thinking so that your business isn't vulnerable.

The internet has also peeled off a layer of obscurity from businesses. With so much information available to us, consumers have come to expect transparency. Now companies must be very open about services and pricing because consumers expect no less. To make matters complicated, not only do they have to keep pace with the internet and provide transparency, but they also have to worry about getting bigger or getting bought out. Additionally, they have to learn to play tough in a competition-free zone. How can you possibly create a competition-free zone on the internet, you might wonder? After all, it offers so many more options for clients, making most businesses appear a small fish in a large ocean. The answer is you can create this competition-free zone by offering wisdom over knowledge.

It's like chess, which I played competitively when I was growing up. Today there is a computer that can beat the best chess masters in the world every time because it has knowledge that a human being couldn't. This caused a disruption in the world of chess, so to speak. Similarly, the internet disrupted the marketplace. And the businesses that continued to be successful are the ones that gravitated to *wisdom*, not to knowledge.

But to apply wisdom over knowledge, you must understand the difference between the two terms. Knowledge is basically just information. It can be obtained from books or podcasts or blogs or national publications or the internet. Most anyone nowadays has access to knowledge.

Wisdom on the other hand is not only about IQ but also EQ or your emotional quotient, where you're able to recognize and respond wisely to emotions. It's about social quotient and how well you get along with people and also about adversity quotient or how good you are at dealing with problems and obstacles. I first heard this from Bernie Stoltz, and it makes so much sense.

By cultivating these different components of wisdom within you, you can create a competition-free zone or, better yet, become a disrupter.

The medical industry saw disruption when insurance companies lowered reimbursements doctors received for procedures. Most doctor's offices decided just to make less money and continue operating exactly as they were. Yet their costs were going up year after year, shooting sky high. Soon, they grew less and less happy showing up to work every day, until finally they realized how miserable they were, threw in the towel, and admitted they were caught in a dead-end career. Meanwhile, the best and brightest grew exponentially. Some created their own in-house insurance plans and figured out ways to enhance quality and go fee-for-service, where patients pay out of pocket instead of going through insurance.

If medical speak is a bit alien to you, consider the limousine industry in the age of Uber. The best of the best limousine companies offer a caliber of service Uber cannot match. They don't focus on airport rides or weddings. Instead, they focus on having their fleet of luxury cars idling at the best hotels so that executives who desire a certain level of exclusivity and luxury can have access to it. What these people get with a limousine service that they don't with Uber is white-glove treatment and a gentleman in a crisp suit opening the door and extending an air of respect while catering to your comforts. Again, the limousine industry is another example of one that has responded to disruption.

Even in our industry, we see many investment and insurance products becoming commoditized. Where a few decades ago there were only a handful of options to choose from when it came to investments and insurance, now you have a whole smorgasbord of them. You can go with a number of products and solutions and through a whole host of people who tout themselves as insurance brokers and financial experts. So what's not being commoditized? Taking a personal, one-on-one approach showing clients how all of the various moving pieces of their business and personal lives need to be integrated. This is important and worth it to spend time doing because for most people, one plus one equals not two but one and a half, which means they're shortchanging themselves from the results they could be achieving. We want our clients to experience one plus one equals three—so they're getting the maximum output from their input. That's the formula for wisdom. If you can help clients achieve their maximum potential, you've created immense value for them. And then you're not as vulnerable to disruption.

The business owners who fail to change tactics and insist on doing work the same way they did ten, twenty, or thirty years ago are the most vulnerable to disruption because they grow so stagnant in their ways that they fail to learn how to change. They're not as adaptable. They're analogous to taxi drivers in the world of Ubers: outdated, overlooked, and forgotten. So how can these people change or adapt to keep up with disruption? Hire the right people around them and surrender some of what they used to do to someone with a fresher outlook who has a greater capacity to adapt and change.

But change can be hard—whether doing it yourself or relinquishing power to someone else so they can drive that change—especially when you're nestled in a comfort zone where you're making plenty of money. Sure, maybe you're not making as much as you should be but enough to where there's no pain, so you feel that forcing or adapting to change is pointless. But refusing to change could also be as simple as keeping an employee who doesn't adhere to your core values because you feel they're "good enough." The detriment to just hanging on and sailing by in the day to day without evolving and adapting to disruption is that you end up not changing until you're forced to. And oftentimes by then it's too late.

The other thing you should focus on are the types of relationships you're building and fostering. So let's talk about that a bit.

TRANSFORMATIONAL, NOT TRANSACTIONAL

One thing I would say is that instead of being transaction focused, start being transformation focused. Start with a repeatable process. We talked about McDonald's earlier, and it's worth mentioning again. Because they would not have sold the billions of hamburgers they advertise if every time a customer came, the burgers were made differently or if they had a chance of being a hit or a miss. Consistency is critical. You must have a process you can repeat and teach.

Next, you've got to have efficiency in your back office. You've got to trim the fat from your business. You've got to figure out a way to compete with or disrupt the big players.

For instance, rarely do any accounting firms in the country do taxes anymore. What I mean by that is that they use software systems to complete tax returns. So why hire these firms if they're simply charging you to plug your information into a software you yourself could purchase? What's the benefit? The answer is that these companies are no longer selling just tax returns. They are selling advice. They're selling wisdom.

In our firm, too, we've gone from transactional to transformational. Our business has gone from selling investments to selling advice, strategy, and wisdom. We personalize each component to create an experience for our clients. Sure, when you do this, it could be that you end up losing the people who are looking only for a transactional relationship with you. But in today's world, where business has become so impersonal, there's still a great need for transformational, not transactional, relationships, with plenty of clients seeking exactly that. They are looking for a relationship where people, loyalty, and experience count. As a business, that's what you should focus on providing.

However, the business mindset most business owners have is to catch the highest number of fish possible. Often in the process, we fail to recognize that there are still plenty of fish in the sea. So you don't have to, and shouldn't, cater your business to the lowest common denominator. In other words, don't chase after clients who would abandon you if you raised prices a quarter of a cent. That's running a commodity, not a business. But there's more to life than just running a business. Along those lines, I want to touch on another very important point and share a personal story.

FOCUS IN THE NOW

My grandfather worked his whole life. At sixty-five he planned an incredible retirement from his position as chairman of the board of Christian Dior. But then two months before his retirement, he passed away. I was just a young boy at the time, but this story still somehow affected me deeply as I grew older. I realized that we never know what will happen or when, so it's crucial to enjoy life—before it's too late.

Part of living a good, fulfilling life you can enjoy is learning new things and creating new capabilities, not doing the same old things in the same old ways over and over again on repeat.

In high school I worked on an assembly line at Birmingham Sound Reproducers turntable company. I earned $4.04 an hour doing the same function every day in the assembly line. I remember thinking, "Oh my god! If I have to do this for another twenty-five years, I'll go crazy."

The following summer I ran the assembly line, and then I did some work in the office. Every summer I learned new capabilities, which enabled me to continue to grow. I knew if I fell into the trap of doing the same thing year after year, I would have been bored to tears. So that simply wasn't an option.

Little did I realize at the time that I already had the entrepreneurial mindset. Slowly, I put this very mindset to use when I became a business owner and then an investor. I learned to keep evolving, start delegating things that didn't require me or my time in specific and made sure to value every moment I had by maximizing how I was spending my time—every moment in the present. In choosing this path of learning and growth, I felt I was already doing justice to the memory of my grandfather. I was working hard to create a quality of life that I could hopefully still be around to enjoy before it was too late. You can too.

YOU'RE NOT PAYING FOR ADVICE; YOU'RE PAYING FOR WISDOM

When I was a kid, I remember watching football with keen interest. Often, one phrase I'd catch the announcers say repeatedly was "You gotta take what the defense gives you." At the time I thought it was the stupidest thing I'd ever heard. I don't want to take what anyone gives me, I thought. I want to take what I want.

When I grew up and entered the business world, I heard another saying I thought was stupid: "All I want is a level playing field." And I thought to myself, but I don't want a level playing field. I want to run straight downhill—and till this day, I still do. I want to run in a competition-free zone where our business is the only place a client can get a certain experience.

One of those experiences, a while back, had to do with my near-photographic memory, but then computers and the internet came along and ruined that advantage. The experience I offered was coming up with unique facts and information most people didn't know. I used to try to be the smartest guy in the room. Today Google has me beat. Everyone has smartphones they can look up things on.

The internet has changed every business, including ours, so that people are no longer paying for knowledge. After all, to gain knowledge, all they have to do is launch YouTube or go to Google. What they're paying for today is what no computer in the world can help create: wisdom. One advantage we humans still have over our robotic counterparts is that computers can't anticipate or handle human emotions or replicate the feeling of protecting or taking care of someone, and they certainly can't replace the joy of collaboration with a team. Sure, my photographic memory isn't as useful as it once was, but I've found other ways to serve my clients best.

When I started my business in 1985, I didn't start it to only make money, although we've certainly done that too. It was our vehicle to make other people's lives better. But our clients didn't want knowledge—there are many places to get that—they wanted what few places can offer: wisdom. What's wisdom? The ability to anticipate the future.

Personally and professionally, a part of wisdom is also being able to understand and control emotions around money.

FOMO AND EMOTIONAL DECISIONS ABOUT FINANCES

Most people think that money and finances are math, but money is actually psychological. And the advantage humans have over computers when it comes to psychology is that computers can't understand how humans may react. For instance, when it comes to the stock market, people want to buy low and sell high. But psychologically, they end up buying high and selling low because when the market goes crazy, they get a strong bout of FOMO—fear of missing out. So when they see the numbers spiking and people getting rich, they want in on the fortune. Before you know it, when the market is at its peak, they're throwing their money in the bucket, too, so they don't miss out on something great. Then when the market crashes and they read the newspaper, turn on the TV, or talk to their neighbors, they think, "Oh my God! The world is ending." The market has dropped 30 or 40 or 50 percent, and they think, "There goes my retirement!" And then they sell.

People make financial decisions based on emotion. Sure, a computer can give you logic, but financial advisors help ensure that emotion never trumps logic. They help ensure you're making solid long-term decisions.

Sometimes clients will say they have no money to save for retirement or to put toward their children's college tuition. So I'll point out, "Well, you got a $10,000 tax refund last year. What did you do with it?" Turns out, they bought themselves a fancy watch because a government refund is, to them, free money. I ask them, what's the difference between putting away $800 a month or saving your tax refund? Won't the bank accept both types of deposits?

In divorces especially, people tend to make rash decisions grounded in emotion instead of logic. Perhaps they want revenge, or they want material things that don't really matter. That's where the human brain comes in handy over a computer's intelligence, and I steer them toward what really matters. Yet messy divorces aren't the only time emotions can get in the way of logic. Sometimes people do the opposite and put their faith in love when they're newly married. Don't get me wrong. I'm a romantic at heart and I believe in fairy tales, but I also believe that you should have a plan for your partnership with your spouse. Because life is never predictable and things can take a turn for the worse, no matter how much we wish to believe they couldn't or won't happen that way with us.

When we plan properly with wisdom and trust in experienced advisors, great things can happen, not by happenstance but because we were prepared. As a financial advisor, I help ensure that no matter what happens in clients' lives, we find a way to change the trajectory of their futures.

When we plan properly with wisdom and trust in experienced advisors, great things can happen, not by happenstance but because we were prepared.

Think about the Kardashians for a moment. No, really! I used to think of them as a car wreck, but look at them from this lens of strategic planning and anticipating for the future, and Kris Jenner is nothing short of brilliant. Ask yourself for a moment what this family started off being famous for. Robert Kardashian had hidden evidence in the O. J. Simpson murder case, and Kim Kardashian made a sex tape. In another time these actions would have brought disgrace upon their family. They would have been shunned and insulted in society. But Kris Jenner saw these early exposures not as a downfall but as an opportunity to open doors for her family. And that's exactly what she did—in the form of a multibillion-dollar net worth. That takes planning. That shows wisdom. Business smarts aside, there's more to what can make you a sensation in your industry. For this, I'd like to venture back to our earlier topic of cultivating an environment where you are it—your competitors can't touch you.

CREATING A COMPETITION-FREE ZONE

We've talked a bit now about cultivating a competition-free zone. It sounds ideal. No competition, just you on not an even playing field but rather on a downward slope where you are free to run at top speed with no one impeding your progress. But how do you achieve this ideal zone?

It's important to analyze your strengths and also what your alleged competitors are doing. In this discovery process, you might learn that either you need to acquire additional capabilities, or you've got to be willing to do something different that your competitors are either not willing or able to do. In other words, you've got to flip the script.

To paint a better picture, I'll ask you to consider this: Imagine you're on an airplane, flying first class, and the person you're sitting next to asks you what you do for a living. The moment you answer, chances are, they'll pigeonhole you into a box based on your industry type, assuming that all financial advisors/lawyers/consultants, etc. are the same. Your job then becomes to find a way to distinguish yourself so it's near impossible for them to categorize you with the rest. In other words, create your own box where only you can fit. How do you do this? It's only accomplished after you figure out how your competitors treat their clients that you can then create an experience that's second to none.

Everybody tells me how much their customers and clients and patients love them, but to me, if you're doing what your competitors are doing, you're just another wolf in the pack. What are you willing to do to flip the script and create an experience for that person that is second to none? Consider this: Every time I'm in La Jolla, California, I go to a restaurant called George's. What's so impressive about George's is that they confirm the reservation several times, their waitstaff is genuinely nice to me, and both the owner and the maître d' visit my table. Plus, the food is great. There's a number of really extraordinary restaurants in this country, and we've all got our favorites, but what George's does differently is they call me the day after my reservation to ask me how my experience was. Who else does that? So I'm a George's fan. You couldn't get me to go to another restaurant in town if you tried. Be a George's. Ask yourself how you're unique, remarkable, and therefore memorable. That's what creates your competition-free zone.

Creating a competition-free zone isn't new to me. It's something I've practiced for decades. In 1990 I had a cell phone, which was a rare novelty back then. And I could barely afford the $4,000 bill each month. Phones were giant and heavy back then, and when you held them, you looked like you could be commanding operations and military missions in Iraq. They were nothing like the light smartphones of nowadays. So why did I invest on this exorbitant splurge? Because back then everyone in my business had their clients call into the office, and then maybe at the end of the day or the next day, they would check their messages and call back. But by making this hefty investment each month, I was ensuring that *my* clients had instantaneous access to me. Having a cell phone and offering this exclusive real-time access to me was a competitive advantage for me for a good five years or so before most people in my industry caught up and bought their own cell phones too.

Then I got a RIM pager, which allowed you to send and receive messages over the internet via a wireless network back when texting didn't exist. Once again, my clients had instantaneous access to me in another medium at a time when many people still didn't have email. (And if they did, it was through the computer in their office.) So again, I created another competition-free zone for another three or four years until email and texting entered center stage as the norm.

Now, of course, everyone has access to everything: phone, text, email, etc. Yet I am obsessed, still, with answering calls and messages as quickly as possible. It's what separates me from my competition, and it's really a simple way to create a competition-free zone. After all, you don't have to be a Harvard graduate or have an IQ of 180 to return a phone call or a text or an email. What are the little things that you're going to do that your competition can't or won't to create an experience for your clients? When you learn the answer and apply it is when you enter your competition-free zone. One of the ways to take yourself to a competition-free zone is by changing how your clients see you.

MINDSHIFTS FOR UNCOMMON THINKING

Every year millions of quarter-inch drill bits are sold by manufacturers. But really, the customers of these manufacturers don't need a drill bit. They need a quarter-inch hole in the wall. We ask our clients to have a similar sense of uncommon thinking. And then ultimately, you want to change the way your clients think about things—and about you.

People will always want to talk about how much money they need for retirement, but the answer financial advisors give usually follows in the form of pablum financial planning most everyone offers. They focus on selling stocks and bonds or insurance instead of helping people live the lives they want. Do you want people to dream as big as they can dream and then put together a plan that takes flight toward that dream? I do. And if you do it right, most of the time, the dream you thought impossible will be more than achieved. In those rare cases where people shoot for the moon and get only the stars, well, heck, they're still better off than where they started—because before that, their dreams had been only earthbound.

An experienced financial advisor is a concierge, guiding you through this incredible, extraordinary journey called life to bend the pathways and clear the brush so you can traipse through life the way you desire.

The biggest mistakes I see business owners make are in their failures to plan and in following along with the pack, doing what everybody else is doing. But when you're running in a dog sled team and you're not the lead dog, the view never changes. Right? Most of the time, the barrier is psychological, a belief that you can't execute the dream. That's why people hire us, to help them execute their goals and ambitions.

Not only do you get a fully laid-out plan, but your advisor also then works with you to anticipate and create game plans for potential barriers that could crop up instead of focusing their efforts solely on identifying which stocks and bonds you should pick. An experienced financial advisor is a concierge, guiding you through this incredible, extraordinary journey called life to bend the pathways and clear the brush so you can traipse through life the way you desire. And let's face it, we all know everyone has desires and dreams, so it's important we touch on how to achieve those dreams and remove any obstacles on the path toward them.

LIFTING BARRIERS TO YOUR LIFE DREAMS

Many people outsource their finances without taking into consideration their own dreams. But it's a con because handling finances is and truly should be a full-contact team sport. The best way to tackle it is to roll up your sleeves and get a team of powerful advisors who take into consideration how you envision your life to be in the next ten years. Your input is crucial—you cannot be a backseat passenger leaving the steering wheel of your life at the hands of someone else with minimal, if any, input from you.

Too often, people fall in love with an asset, so they put 100 percent of their money into, say, real estate. But then the real estate market breaks bad on them and interest rates rise, and before they know it, they're bankrupt. Or they fall in love with a stock or a sector and think, "Oh, this company's technology stock is only going to go up!" So they put all their money there, and then the market crashes.

Occasionally, the barriers come from people around you. We've come up against family members and friends of our clients who don't want them to get too successful. It's like crabs in a bucket trying to escape, clawing at each other and dragging one another down—whether from jealousy or fear, who knows—and preventing a single one from scaling toward freedom.

As financial advisors, all we do is furnish a permission slip. This slip is basically the support, wisdom, and guile to say that you can be anything you want to be. When it comes down to it, we find most people are seeking the following three things:

1. Direction with a clear path along the journey.

2. Creativity, but it's gotta be mom and apple pie. It can't be any scams or schemes.

3. An advisor who is going to be there every step along the way.

As I mentioned earlier, I believe too many advisors talk too much and listen too little. I have a process for asking powerful questions that help uncover my clients' true needs. For instance, I'll ask, "What's the name of your attorney or your accountant?" Then I'll ask, "If you had an important life decision, not a legal question or a tax question, would these people be one of your first two phone calls?" Finally, I ask, "If I was moving into the area and looking for a great attorney or accountant, would you highly recommend them to me?" Then I listen.

I find I am a better listener when I'm not talking. Sometimes when I'm on a phone call, the person on the other end might pause and ask, "Are you still here?" I'm so busy listening and taking notes they're not sure I'm even there. But today that's a valued skill because most people are too busy thinking about what they're going to say next versus actively listening.

Once you're able to use the advice I've shared to become cognizant of and lift the barriers around you, it's time to go all in, heart and soul.

COMMITMENT MATTERS

Malcolm Gladwell said to create mastery, you must have ten thousand hours of experience. Well, now I have over a hundred thousand hours of experience, and I help people play in a place where there is less competition, doing things that their competitors are often not willing to do. And I teach other advisors to do the same. Not only that, I teach them another critical lesson: to combine the experience they have with commitment. The formula of experience plus commitment will never serve you wrong. And commitment always gives you an edge in life. Again, what are you willing to give up to have what you don't already?

For example, when I was in my twenties, I had a very wealthy client hire me as his financial advisor. When I asked why he had chosen to work with me when he could have gone to anyone else, he said it was because he had called my office and I called him back within a half an hour from Hawaii. So I jest with new financial advisors, advising them to always tell their clients that they're calling from Hawaii!

Jokes aside, people sense when you're serving their best interests instead of your own. They sense that it's not only what you produce but also that you're willing to do anything to make their lives better. They want to feel you are committed to them. And in the end, they're paying for wisdom, not advice.

LIVE WITH YOUR BACK AGAINST THE WALL

....

It never ceases to amaze me how ill-prepared people can be when something bad happens. It's as though they think that nobody around them can ever get sick or die. Nobody can go bankrupt. Nobody can get sued. Of course, we don't want to spend our lives planning for bad things to happen, but we should anticipate them, nevertheless.

This is especially important for entrepreneurs, who are among the most susceptible to downturns, because it's generally their capital that's on the line if life ever turns sour—their skin in the game. So when life gets disrupted for an entrepreneur, it can become cataclysmic.

The saying goes "ready, aim, fire," and yet so many entrepreneurs conduct themselves in a scrambled order of "fire, ready, aim." They act, then prepare themselves, then try to fix things. In other words, they put their efforts behind reactionary tasks instead of delegating chores to their employees, their kitchen cabinet (more about this in a minute), or other experienced professionals.

Let's say I want to decorate my home. I'd "ready" by hunting for decorators, "aim" by hiring the best one, and "fire" by collaborating my sensibilities to their expertise so they can execute on the vision. I want them to show me what they're envisioning because they're the best at what they do, and it's not my area of expertise. This would make for a solid collaboration between an experienced professional and me, their client. That frees my time, empowering me to concentrate on my own work.

But again, that doesn't mean planning for the worst should be a concept reserved just for entrepreneurs. Everyone should plan—the self-employed, business owners, employees, investors, any of us and all of us.

In 2001 I was living in Summit, New Jersey, when the World Trade Center was attacked. That September morning, about a dozen cars were in the train station parking lot. They remained there that night but also the next night and the night after. The implication was heart-shattering to me. Some of those young, affluent Wall Street families whose loved ones those cars belonged to no doubt had recently received the worst news of their lives. Later, they were forced to move out of town into condos or townhouses, their lives altered in ways that proper planning could have helped mitigate.

Most of us have lived through such events or at the very least are privy to how fast life can take a sudden, fatal turn. Yet so many people still forgo doing the proper legal work to develop strong wills and trusts to leave behind for their loved ones. They don't have asset protection, exposing their families to creditors and lawsuits. I know this personally, having paid millions of dollars in alimony, child support, and equitable distribution. Before I got married, I didn't have a prenuptial agreement. If I had, it would have saved me a lot of aggravation and a lot of cash, but I had no anticipation of getting divorced (we always think it will never happen to us), and now the only way I can get out of alimony is by keeling over dead!

Similarly, people go into business agreements without a clear understanding of both parties' expectations, which is basically the same thing as getting married without a prenup. Again, we think, I know this person, we're good together, what could possibly go wrong? But things do go wrong, so it's important to have proper planning that's both coordinated and integrated. That's why my friend and colleague, divorce attorney Susan Reach Winters, takes the team approach when working with her clients. She created a team that includes herself (an attorney), myself (a financial advisor), a forensic accountant, and a family therapist. With this remarkable team in place, Susan and her clients play in a competition-free zone, and her clients get a high-quality experience.

Your legal documents, asset protections, and ownership should all be integrated. This is no time to save money on accounting, legal advice, or insurance because that can lead to problems. I know because I've seen it. For instance, one person put all their companies under one umbrella, only to have that one company take them all down because of a lawsuit. Investing in proper planning is an investment in your future. In the same way that planning for the worst is a necessity, so is surrounding yourself with the best people who will keep you propped up, which is what we'll talk about next.

ASSEMBLE YOUR KITCHEN CABINET

It's important to assemble the best team for your needs in the moment and beyond. When I was in my thirties and my business was still new, I wanted to be around great business developers. In my forties, when my business was growing, I needed a good lawyer. Now that I'm in my fifties, the most important thing is my health because if I lack energy or get sick or hurt, it will affect my ability to perform. So now I surround myself with the best doctors. These different resources make up what I like to call my proverbial "kitchen cabinet."

So now my question to you is, who makes up your "kitchen cabinet"? What I mean is, who are the folks you've assembled around you that you not only respect but also fully trust? Who can give you the right advice when you need it most?

Not everybody feels comfortable assembling a team. I have clients who like to keep their cards close to the vest; they don't establish relationships they'll need when the going gets tough. They don't trust anybody, and perhaps that's because they've been burned before. Or perhaps, like most entrepreneurs, they're simply too busy building their businesses through blood and sweat, toiling up to one hundred hours a week with just themselves to rely on. With so many hours constantly spent on their business, they often don't have time to cultivate and assemble a team, even if they want to. But a team is essential to surviving the downturns of business and life. And just as important is anticipating what's ahead—our next topic.

PREPARING FOR THE PUNCHES

Most people react, but the best anticipate, which is why we try to help people peek around corners when we can. What do I mean by that? What I said earlier—life ends up happening when we least expect it. Divorce, illness, losing a loved one, a pandemic, inflation, a recession—basically, the things that we often don't expect or anticipate or ever think will happen to us. How we try to help people peek around the corner is by employing some basic but effective, distinct asset protection strategies to make sure that clients are protected from these unpleasant yet often unavoidable surprises.

Because at the end of the day, you should be preparing for contingencies. When you prepare for the unexpected, you grow empowered to survive some of the darkest storms. True there are times you can't completely navigate every circumstance, but if anything, you'll be properly prepared and often come out stronger, at least. And most importantly, in almost every case, you'll have survived. The price of success is paid in advance.

I want to clarify something here. Just because life can "happen" doesn't mean we stop living it. I don't stop going swimming in the ocean because there's a chance I could be devoured by a shark. I don't stop going outside when it's raining because there's a possibility that I might get struck by lightning. Find the balance between living your life and being prepared—that's my job and the job of the people at my firm: to help people navigate situations the best we can.

That's why I'm not only a financial advisor but also a key business strategist who uses critical thinking. I'm not clairvoyant, but I can help anticipate and prepare for the ups and downs of building a business.

When it comes to preparation, we can look to sports for inspiration. The best sports coaches don't win the game on game day. They win the game in practice on the courts the week before. Similarly, I've learned that, in our business, it's always the preparation, preparation, preparation—physical and mental—that gets you successfully to the finish line. Be prepared for whatever comes your way—hurdles, obstacles, fires—believing you'll find a way to get through it, get around it, and get up from it.

That's why my mantra is if I get knocked down, I get back up. If I get knocked down again, I will get up again. If I get knocked down a third time, I'll keep getting up and keep getting up. The victory of life is just continuing to be able to get back up.

One of the keys to life is making sure that your future is bigger and brighter than your past, but if you let a setback take you down, you can't make that bigger, brighter life. We all know that one person who faced an adversity that they never quite recovered from. Chances are, you also know entrepreneurs who got caught up in the chaos of life, getting their head buried in the day-to-day minutiae and ended up working themselves to death.

Again, as financial advisors, our job is to pull your head out of the sand bucket. We want to help clients move away from buying a job to owning a business. We want to have them get paid for their intellectual property, which they can use to build wealth, so they don't have to be in the salt mines one hundred hours a week. Remember, money is not math; it's psychological. So if you don't have a plan in place to get through tough times, you may struggle, and that will affect your financial stability. Continuing on in the vein of the psychological mind, I think it's important we hit on another relevant topic—how to use your mental abilities to their best.

THE MAGICAL ELIXIR OF SUCCESS

Ninety percent of life is mental, but it's also how you use your mental abilities that makes a difference. Take the movie and the book *The Secret*, which was released in 2006. It was about the law of attraction, the idea that if you think good things, good things will happen. I like positive thinking, and I'm a fan of Tug McGraw's quote from the 1973 Mets: "Ya gotta believe." But I'd argue that this law must also be paired with a solid action plan. Think about it this way: if someone's breaking into my house, I'd like to have the belief that everything's going to be okay, but I'd also love to have a gun.

We have taken on clients who run businesses without business plans and clients who want to be financially independent but have no financial plan. We tell them it starts with a belief that things can get better, which leads to confidence—not bravado or hubris but a quiet, steely confidence that they're going to be able to accomplish their goals.

Still, nothing replaces hard work, particularly for an entrepreneur. So if you have a belief that leads to confidence and then you're willing to put hard work into it, that's the magic elixir. You can't have just one component or the other; rather, you need a healthy dose of both to get things going in a good direction.

And yet the power of your thoughts and your mind are far stronger than your ability to act. Entrepreneurs need to think about how they could get paid from the work of others and delegate work to obtain leverage. Once you shift your mentality from seeking payment for what you know, not for what you do, you shift from owning a job to owning a business.

Think of it in terms of retirement. Most people in physical blue-collar roles retire after twenty-five years because they

Once you shift your mentality from seeking payment for what you know, not for what you do, you shift from owning a job to owning a business.

can't scale their jobs. If you're a fireman, you can't keep on climbing ladders and running through burning buildings into old age. So you retire. But if you're, say, a psychiatrist, you could hit the peak of your powers well after retirement age. However, when you retire, all of the clapping stops, all of the teamwork stops, and all of the excitement ends.

Similarly, an entrepreneur never retires from their thinking, their creativity, or their business expansion. Yet I'm still most often approached by entrepreneurs who like to discuss how soon they can retire because they're tired of the grind. In fact, many entrepreneurs out there are miserably unhappy in business. But that's because they're not making the best use of what they could be doing and how they could be doing it. My job is to help them get paid for what they've created, shifting them from owning a job to owning a business and then into being an investor. That's when they get excited, so excited that they suddenly never want to retire. And when someone, like a client, puts their confidence in you, I always say the aim should be abundance.

INTRODUCING ABUNDANCE

When I'm the experienced professional for someone else, I am honored that they've trusted and chosen and invited me into their experience. My small role in that experience is the most rewarding thing I can think of because for me the gift is always in the giving and sharing. And in that comes another great blessing: being able to introduce abundance in the lives of others. This can be in the form of money or time or confidence. It's all relevant to what that individual wants out of life.

Once you start to introduce abundance into people's lives, it's contagious. You want to do it more and more and more. Because suddenly, everything goes from being difficult or impossible for that person to being completely possible. And instead of focusing on what they don't want from life, you get them to a point where they spend their energy focusing on what they do want. That's when we put together a plan to help them achieve their dreams and live their best life.

I had this epiphany in my early thirties when I was shadowing a managing partner of a large international accounting firm. Being in his company, I realized that I didn't want to be "just" a financial advisor. I wanted to be a businessman too. I saw how this gentleman ran his business, and I realized that when you create value, the world beats a path to your door.

But it's also important to acknowledge that not everybody's path is the same. Some people need to make mistakes to learn. We can only hope that they're small mistakes. When we make mistakes we apologize, clean up the mess, and make sure it doesn't happen again. When these amazing people are ready for abundance, my firm and I are here to act as their concierge, consigliere, friend, brother, and/or mentor along the journey. It's never my journey, and I'm not putting my sensibility or my plan into theirs. Rather, I'm helping them create their own journey by sharing my wisdom. And being on the receiving end of that level of experience can be life-altering, which is what we'll talk about next.

TURBOCHARGING LIFE

When you have strong support and experience behind you, it can be like a turbocharger in your life that propels you to places you never thought you could possibly go. Often, it's not till many years later that you learn that you've somehow, in some way, served as that very turbocharger for someone else just by being kind or helpful at a critical moment.

One of my earliest, most significant memories of being turbo-charged is from high school. I was too immature at the time and I didn't realize it until years later. My history teacher at the time—a man named Lloyd Jaeger—believed in me fully, but I think he knew I wasn't working to my full capacity or, as I'd call it, to my highest and best use. At the time I couldn't understand why he seemed to be tougher on me than he was on the rest of my classmates. Back then his approach toward me seemed almost aggressive and entirely unnecessary. And because I couldn't understand why he was different toward just me, it annoyed me. At the same time, the challenge was exhilarating and made for among the best times of my life because I came to realize that I wasn't competing against other people, but rather, I was competing against my own abilities.

Mr. Jaeger's approach drove me to always try to work to my fullest potential. But the true gift he left me with was the understanding that I could be the very best version of myself and still be the biggest cheerleader for someone else, even if we were in competition with one another. I learned I could be happy for someone else, be a great friend to them, be their fiercest cheerleader, and also serve as inspiration, even if superficially we may be competing—all because I'm confident in myself and in knowing I've done all I can to do and be my very best. That's what it means to live in a competition-free zone. However, no matter how good you might have it, remember, you're still a dog—an underdog.

BE THE UNDERDOG

No matter how successful I've gotten, I always think of myself as an underdog because I believe that's how you can prevent yourself from growing content or lazy. Never buying into the mindset or belief that you're "all that" keeps you on your toes. Besides, even if you end up buying into your own hype and thinking you are all that, the world has a brutal way of giving you a reality check to remind you that you're actually *not*. It might knock you gently at first, but ignore the first one and the subsequent knocks only grow heavier. By the third or fourth knock, you're all but kicked off your feet with your face in the dust. Unfortunately, that's what it takes for realization to strike some people.

When you consider yourself an underdog, however, you never take anything for granted. No success, no accomplishment, no task is insignificant or too small. If I'm going to give my clients—both new and established—my all, they deserve for me to be at my very best and to give them everything I've got. To do that and remain humble and never take any of them for granted, I adopt the mindset of an underdog, which is humility paired with confidence.

Dwayne "The Rock" Johnson calls it living with your back against the wall. No matter how well he does, no matter how much fame and fortune he has to his name, he makes it a point to always remind himself where he came from—evicted as a teenager with nowhere to live and arrested for fighting and theft. Now among the highest-paid actors with a net worth north of $800 million[2], he still lives like an underdog and never loses sight of his roots—a practice all of us, especially business owners, can learn from.

---

2   Allie Nelson, "Baller Indeed! Dwayne Johnson's Net Worth Went From Seven Bucks to Superhero Heights!," Parade.com, July 28, 2022, https://parade.com/celebrities/dwayne-johnson-net-worth

NEVER MAJOR IN MINOR THINGS

Entrepreneurs and people who aspire to be entrepreneurs work so hard that it's usually rare to have to even question their efforts—because their commitment is often 100 percent behind their businesses. For them, the problem isn't the number of hours that they put in but the efficiency with which they handle their business. One commonly similar attribute among them is that they tend to major in minor things, spending hours on tactics that do not move the needle for their business.

If you tie up your time all day, trudging home exhausted after an eight-, ten-, twelve-, fourteen-, or sixteen-hour day, you might feel like you've accomplished a lot. After all, you're pulling long hours, committing the most valuable resource you have—time—to your business, and working to give it your all. But what most entrepreneurs don't realize is that if you didn't spend those exorbitant number of hours focusing on the important things, your business will remain as stagnant as a duck in water. Like many entrepreneurs, if you're not focused on the issues that truly matter in all those hours spent working and if you're failing to differentiate between urgent and unimportant, you're essentially wasting your time.

For instance, say your cell phone rings and you answer, even though you don't recognize the number. Whoever is on the line now has your attention. Sure, it might be somebody who's crucial to your business success, but it could just as easily also be the dry cleaners reminding you to pick up your clothes. Or a telemarketer. Either way, that person, whoever they are, still have the benefit of your attention in the middle of your workday.

If you don't create rules and boundaries for your employees or your family, allowing yourself to be constantly interrupted all day, every day, by whomever so chooses, you'll never get around to doing the work required of you. The problem here is that you've failed to create an environment, structure, or process so that people know how to reach you without being a disruption.

When whoever's in front of you can have your attention at their whim, regardless of whether or not they deserve to be the most important thing in that moment, their issue automatically becomes the center of your attention. Operating in this way by the seat of your pants where your attention can be claimed so easily is not your highest and best use. Another important point to focus on right alongside how and when you allocate attention is your emotional acuity.

EMOTIONAL FITNESS FOR LEADERS

I'd say single-handedly the most important thing entrepreneurs can do is to take care of their minds. Emotional fitness is paramount because when you're the leader of an organization, people watch what you do and say very carefully. And when a business owner is erratic, when the heartbeat of the organization is reactionary, the business itself won't have emotional fitness. And all of that depends on and stems and flows from a single place: your own emotional fitness. As a business owner, it's integral that you be the calming, steadying influence because that's what drives confidence from employees and clients alike.

There's a well-known Hispanic food company called Goya, and years ago I stole a great idea from my longtime friend and partner Nat Perlmutter. Legend (really myth!) has it at our office that if I'm unhappy with your work, I'll put a can of Goya beans at your desk. And that would be a signal that you're not working hard enough—because Goya stands for "get off your ass."

What isn't myth is that I keep a can of Goya beans at my own desk every day. Any passersby who don't know this story most likely assume I'm in love with Spanish food or have an unhealthy obsession with beans.

But really, it's my signal to everyone at my company that we'll never grow complacent and that there's nothing we won't do as an organization to keep hustling to make the lives of every single person we touch better. In order to keep to this mission and goal, I must remain emotionally fit. My job is to make other people believe what I believe.

But how do you foster emotional fitness within yourself? To be emotionally fit, you must always be present in the moment, no matter how you're feeling. Even if you're having a bad day, you have to have a little Zen in you and breathe through any issues. There have been times when I've gone three or four nights in a row without good sleep, putting me on edge. Or there have been times when I've been in a heavy argument with a family member. Even in those challenging moments, I still have to show up confident and composed enough to create and foster a level of emotional fitness throughout the organization.

Often, you'll find that dysfunctional companies are run by dysfunctional owners. Yet they insist on bringing in a consultant or a coach, throwing money at them, and insisting, "You don't need to fix me. You need to fix everybody in my organization." But if only they tried the reverse, if only they realized that with a little emotional fitness, *they'd* be fixed, and then the organization would automatically follow suit.

For my readers who understand chiropractic care, you could best compare this philosophy to the technique called upper cervical chiropractic. In this technique the focus is on adjusting the top two bones in the neck, the atlas and the axis. The theory is that when you align these two vertebrae at the top of the spine, all the others will automatically snap into place and line up.

Businesses operate much the same way. If you can get a business owner and the company's leaders to align their emotional fitness, you'll have an emotionally aligned organization, too, and then you can focus on achievement.

As another example, there's an expression that says you can't give what you don't have. Or you may have also heard that you can't fill from an empty cup. So what you've got to do is first create within yourself whatever it is you're looking to feed into the universe. In this case foster emotional fitness first in yourself, and then you can create it across your organization. Let's talk a little bit more about what emotional fitness actually is.

Emotional fitness is about discipline. It's about being in control of your emotions and using them in a positive way with those around you. But let's face it. There are times in life where it's near impossible to control your emotions. Maybe your dog got run over or you're at the brink of divorce. Maybe your child is about to move out and make you an empty nester. Life is rife with emotions, so expecting you to be a hundred percent in control of yours at all times is tough, if not impossible. What do we do in those situations?

When you're angry or upset, I believe the twenty-four-hour rule is brilliant to live by—wait twenty-four hours before responding. Sometimes when I find myself feeling like I'll explode or lash out at somebody in person, by email or text, etc., I'll sit quietly for a day without responding so I can get a better handle on my emotions. When I'm calmer is when I reply.

The other thing I'll often do is write out an email that captures all my frustration, anger, and emotion. And then when I'm done, I delete it.

Both of these methods are equally as effective, and by using them, I avoid undue damage to relationships. Most of the time, you'll find that emotional decisions are almost always the wrong decisions.

If you want a simple example, just think of the checkout aisles at any grocery store. There's a reason they're littered with all sorts of knickknacks you probably wouldn't even look at twice if you'd seen them anyplace else in the store. But they're there for a reason because people, usually on impulse, grab these items on a whim as they check out. Sure, they're not expensive items that might break the bank, but they're items that you don't need: a yoyo, a keychain, a piece of candy. You buy these items on impulse. While these are very minuscule decisions made on impulse that won't have a significant impact on your life, the much bigger detrimental decisions made on similar impulse can literally break you or your business.

The other terrible thing about emotional decisions is once you make them and even if later you realize the error of your ways, you end up feeling stuck with that initial decision. In the process you double down on your mistake because now, even though you may secretly know you were wrong, you find yourself having to back up your choice, support it, and move forward with it.

We talked earlier about AQ or adversity quotient. A part of having a high AQ is being able to perform great under stress or extreme emotion—which relates to being emotionally fit.

Of course, regardless of whether you're angry, sad, anxious, or facing any other negative emotion, I've found that the one exercise that never fails to calm and soothe me is breathing. Because breathing is important for emotional fitness.

When a leader is a calming, strong, positive influence and presence, it allows the organization to remain focused on goals by feeding off that energy—and without distractions. But what happens when it's the reverse and you're not emotionally fit? Let's talk about that next because that's an important question.

DO YOU WANT TO BE RESPECTED OR LIKED?

When a leader is not emotionally fit, the organization loses sight of the company's vision and focuses instead on its foibles and weaknesses. This can lead to problems. I'm not saying don't identify problems and try to fix them. But if you continually focus on only the problems, then those will become the center of your organization's attention, which leaves little to no focus on the long-term vision or desired outcome of the company. One of my favorite words is intentionality. Very few things happen by happenstance. In every meeting, I like having an agenda on hand so I can steer the dialogue and achieve a specific outcome. The same should be true of your organization: practice intentionality in everything you do. If you become too emotionally invested in the weeds, you fail to see the big picture and direct your organization in only the way a true leader can.

During the Vietnam War, when an officer led soldiers into very dangerous situations, it mattered greatly whether or not he had the trust and respect of his soldiers. Often, the answer to this question could mean the difference, quite literally, between life or death. Because when officers were not respected or trusted, soldiers would often "frag" them or use fragmentation grenades to kill them so it looked as though they had lost their lives in combat.

In the same way, respect in business is crucial and is in part earned when you have strong bearings over your emotions. But I'm not suggesting you turn into stone or the opposite, bend over backward, making sure every single person in the organization is head over heels in love with you. As a leader, being loved isn't necessary, but you must at least be respected. As the owner of your company, you hold the microphone, so when you speak, your

When a leader is a calming, strong, positive influence and presence, it allows the organization to remain focused on goals by feeding off that energy—and without distractions.

"soldiers" or staff should have enough reverence for you that they trust what you say. That they respect your visions and you as a person. Without this level of respect, you won't earn loyalty or allegiance for yourself, which will only reflect in the outputs of your organization. Ask yourself this: given the opportunity, would your employees do the equivalent of fragging you? If you're not sure or if you have a sneaking suspicion that the answer is yes, it's time to reevaluate how you can earn respect.

Where should you start? With the golden rule, of course: do unto others as you would have them do unto you. Everyone wants respect, but unlike human dignity, this is not something we are all born with or can demand. To earn respect, you must be willing to give respect. Likewise, if you seek kindness, you must first offer it. Again, back to the golden rule: do unto others as you would want done unto you. One way to earn respect among your folks is to learn to look beyond the dollar bill.

MONEY DOESN'T MOTIVATE FOR LONG

One of the key reasons people launch a business is for independence but also because many think that owning your own business can exponentially augment the amount of money you make. I'm not going to tell you that you shouldn't work for money because that sounds a bit counterintuitive. But what I will say is that your vision for yourself investing in a business should go beyond the aspirations of just money. You've got to have a greater reason, a greater purpose. And most importantly your job is to help your employees see your vision, to see that grander purpose so they, too, can realize that your ambitions for your company go beyond dollar bills. The truth is, in the long run, money won't keep people working at peak performance.

Just look at the environment around us. No longer is it that people just want to work for the sake of being fairly compensated. They work so they can have work-life balance. They work so they can feel they're serving a bigger purpose and contributing to something remarkable.

When I launched my business, I always thought I'd make money, but I also thought this company would be my vehicle to making other people's lives extraordinarily better. When I'm keeping emotionally fit is when I'm best able to show my employees that this is not about money. What I mean by that is when I have my emotions in order, I have a clear head that's not influenced by my heart. And when I am in control in this manner, I am able to guide my company and employees to our vision and long-term goals. I am able to take their focus away from just making money or a quick buck because I am stable enough to keep my eyes—and theirs too—on the target: our mission, our vision, or our higher purpose.

Of course, it's great to be successful; it's great to make money. But if it was just about money, you wouldn't see the level of commitment we see in our organization. I'm nearly convinced that some of the younger people in my company don't own a place to live and use the bathroom in the office to wash their faces and brush their teeth because no matter what time of the day or week I come into the office, they're always there working. Now by no means am I condoning becoming a workaholic or encouraging anyone to live and breathe work. The point I'm trying to make here is that these people work with such commitment and ambition not because I'm looking over their shoulders. They're working because they want to create something better, because they're motivated, because they're excited, and because they're thrilled to be a part of something great they feel they can contribute toward.

Dan Sullivan, author of *Who Not How*, says that when people want to create a bigger, better future, not only for themselves but for their clients as well, then they've got something worth working toward. The leader's job is to figure out what motivates each employee because everybody gets motivated by different things, like in the book *The Five Love Languages*. Some of these motivators can apply to employees as well, such as words of affirmation, acts of service, and quality time.

For example, some employees need to feel like they're part of a family (quality time) and some thrive on praise (words of affirmation). If you're in charge, you need to understand this to unleash the very best in the people who work for you. You could be the best general in the world, but with no troops behind you, you aren't really a leader.

The same goes for clients. Some of my clients would be fine if they saw me just once when they first onboarded, while others need me to be practically belly to belly with them every day of our relationship. That doesn't mean that we create special rules for special people. We must follow the rules we've set based on our core values and principles. But if we understand motivation, we can work better with our clients as individuals based on key things they most desire from a business relationship.

But there's more. In addition to whatever most motivates people, you've also got to make sure you run by today's principles and social norms. What you may perceive to be a random act of kindness or a compliment could be misconstrued as something entirely else. You must be cautious about how something that might appear innocent could have some unintended double entendre that may be misinterpreted by the recipient. For example, if you're a male business owner and compliment a female on her sweater, once upon a time, that may have been acceptable. But it very well could be that if your eyes land in the wrong place or if the female feels uncomfortable at your focus on her attire, your "kind" message may miss the mark. That's why it's important to be cognizant of your words and actions.

It's such a diverse world, and people are looking at things from all different viewpoints, which makes it understandable that we don't all hear the same thing. Be sure to make changes in your own behaviors and etiquettes to keep up with the times. And make sure to hire people who can conduct themselves in an adultlike manner, regardless of how diverse they may be from one another in other ideologies, an important point we'll touch on next.

HIRE SELF-MANAGING PEOPLE

Most organizations focus on process, not productivity, and that can be problematic. For a brief time early in my career, I worked for a company where the employees were not committed. Back then we had a typing pool that was responsible for typing all our paperwork. At 4:30 p.m. one Tuesday, I asked the head of the typing pool if someone could type an important document for me. "No" came the reply. "It's going to be done tomorrow."

I pointed out that the office was open until 5:00 p.m., and it wasn't a long document, but it didn't matter. The lady refused to budge. To me, it felt like she was pretty much saying, "I'm here to do a job, and I'm going to do the minimum amount possible to get by."

Culture doesn't trickle up; it trickles down.

Bearing this scenario in mind, when I started my own organization, I focused my energy on what I wanted to achieve. I believe in the expression, "What you think about, you bring about." So when I launched, I was committed to bringing about only the very best. But I also paid attention to what I didn't want. And what I didn't want were employees—I wanted self-managing people who were committed to making clients' lives better. I didn't want people who were just putting in hours from nine to five. We treat our employees like people. If you take care of your people they will take care of your clients. We don't tell them when to take lunch or what hours to work. If they need a mental health day, we expect they won't lie and tell us they're sick. If their sister is in town, we expect them to be honest and take a few days. Our only expectation of them is for them to do their work on time and do it well. Self-managing people can. Once you have these remarkable people in place, your work is not over. It's just beginning. Because now you're tasked with keeping them mesmerized by your vision, an important point I'd be remiss not to address.

BE INSPIRATIONAL AND ASPIRATIONAL

You've got to create an organization in your vision that's not only inspirational but also aspirational. When I say inspirational, I mean that when you talk to people, inspire them so that they're working toward a higher calling and not simply clocking in every day to earn a paycheck. They could feel inspired that they're making a difference in people's lives or somehow making the world a better place through their efforts.

The aspirational part is when they feel they can have an even greater role and add even more value to your organization in trying to fulfill that role.

The best visionaries and the best entrepreneurs inspire their employees and clients. That means they make it so employees appreciate the work they're involved in and clients feel like everyone is working jointly to push them toward a better future state. Sure, it's hard to do that on a consistent basis, but it must be done because when clients feel inspired, they want to stay with you. And when employees feel like they have a purpose and aren't simply a warm body taking up space, it's infinitely easier to have everyone focus relentlessly on pursuing the same goals.

A part of being aspirational is to be able to talk about not only what you're doing now but also what's possible for the future. When your competitors say, "It's too hard. It can't be done," you transform that experience for that client and create more value than anybody else can.

In Gino Wickman's *Traction*, he writes about the Entrepreneurial Operating System® (EOS), a set of concepts and tools designed to help companies implement their vision and get enough traction to grow under a team of functional and healthy leaders. For our organization, it's been transformative.

For a company to get traction, employees must be able to answer yes to all three of Gino's "GWC" questions:

G: Do they get it? In other words, do they understand their role in the company?

W: Do they want it? Are they willing to put in the work to be successful in their job? You shouldn't be there simply because the office is five minutes from your house. You need to believe in the company's vision and want to be there because you feel excited by it.

C: Do they have the capacity to do it? Do they have the mental, physical, and emotional capacities for the job? This is about skills, experience, and emotional fitness.

One of the key challenges companies face with new employees is that they may not have the skills, experience, or capabilities to do their jobs on day one. But leaders must project into the future to determine if their new hires will be able to learn to perform at the right level for the job they're being hired to do.

Sometimes, however, you may come across candidates who really want a position, and despite your hesitations, you end up hiring them—and in the end, you're glad you did because they're phenomenal employees. But as your business becomes more sophisticated, it outgrows their capabilities. Unfortunately, at this point, that means that they don't have the *C* in GWC, which means you'll be forced to get rid of loyal employees, some of whom would practically run through a wall for you. That's painful, especially when you love them and their dedication.

We use a variety of tools, such as the GWC method outlined above, to analyze employees' skills to make sure we put them in the right seats. Wickman also advises you to rate every employee, which helps us determine whether they are indeed where they should be or are lagging. I go down the roster and rate each employee on two things: how well they align with our core values and how capable they are for their role. On an Excel sheet, go person by person, rating each one against these two components, using either a plus sign, a minus sign, or a plus and minus sign.

A plus sign means they meet the component all or most of the time. A plus and minus means they meet it. And if they don't meet it or they don't meet it very often, they get a minus sign. Once I go through and evaluate each individual, I review the results. Those who have one minus or more than two plus minuses probably are not meant for our organization. If I'm conducting this exercise during the hiring part of the process, those symbols are a strong indication that you won't get hired. It might sound tedious to have to go through this exercise, but I promise you it's worth every ounce of effort and time. Because getting as many pluses as possible can make for an extremely powerful organization. I speak from experience. Those pluses mean we are all in alignment. We are well suited to our roles, we are all in sync with our understanding of the company vision, we are all buying into the same culture. We are in near unison, and therefore, we operate like one powerful body of like minds focused on a single goal. And the results from that kind of synchrony and synergy are astounding. It means our culture's right, and if our culture is right, then everything else will take care of itself.

On the other hand, when you bring in the wrong people for the job, it's not only a burden on the organization, but it's also a burden on the person themself. Then the team just loads up work on someone else who will get it done.

Sometimes leaders realize that the reason they're working around the clock until they're practically going to have a stroke yet are still failing to reach their goals is because they do not have the right team beneath them to support them. But they don't change the team because it's easier to stay stagnant or because sometimes they believe that it's too hard to find the right fit for the role.

You've probably heard "a man of a thousand faces." Well, I've seen men and women with a thousand excuses for why the people beneath them are not working to the capacity that the role requires. These leaders are not willing to hold people accountable. But without emotional fitness, you can't hold people accountable anyway. Let me elaborate on what I mean by that.

In this day and age, employees' mindsets have changed drastically from decades ago. Back then, let's say in 1985 to add some context, you worked a hundred hours a week. You might have been verbally and emotionally abused. That was considered to be your rite of passage. If you survived, you became somebody who could make a lot of money and maybe also earn the authority to abuse the next group of people who came in. And on and on it went. In 2022 our private equity and Wall Street firms have learned this: the days of hazing are a distant memory.

Today, especially coming out of the COVID-19 pandemic, the workforce is all about being treated well, attaining work-life balance, wanting to work autonomously, and wanting to work remotely. The challenge for leaders then becomes figuring ways to hold people accountable but to also do it in a way that's effective. Part of that starts with showing them what a great job looks like and then holding them accountable to that standard.

So what does accountability have to do with emotional fitness? Part of emotional fitness when you're trying to hold someone accountable is to make sure that somehow the conversation doesn't turn into something personal or ruled by emotions.

Say, for example, an employee works remotely one day and they don't achieve what you wanted them to by Friday. Suddenly, you're scrambling over the weekend to finish up what they should have days ago. You might feel frustrated, angry, disappointed, upset, tired. Emotional fitness means not letting those feelings overrule you as you sit down and have a conversation with this employee. The wrong approach would be saying, "Hey, Doug, because you didn't do what you were supposed to, I spent all weekend trying to finish this project. I'm so exhausted and upset."

A more productive and emotionally fitness charged conversation would be to hold them accountable to preestablished expectations for their role and host a productive conversation on how they performed (or failed to perform) against those expectations.

When you keep your emotions in check, you're able to better tackle the conversation in a more effective way to hold people to that level of accountability based on fair expectations versus lashing out at them.

But you have to walk the walk if you're going to talk the talk. In other words, if you're holding your employees to certain standards, you can't be a hypocrite. For instance, I get a chuckle when owners of a cash business complain that their employees are stealing money from them, but then they are stealing money from the government by not reporting all their income. Or maybe they show up for work at ten o'clock and then leave for a two-hour lunch. Leaders with emotional fitness do not behave in this manner. And that's why it's important you be a good leader, but also surround yourself by the best ones.

SURROUND YOURSELF WITH LEADERS

Hiring the right leadership team around you is a must. Why? Because you can't expect the soldiers to perform well if the leaders—the captains, the majors, and the generals—who are responsible for heralding the troops are terrible themselves. Great leaders create great followers, but great leaders also create other great leaders. As the ultimate leader, it's in your best interest to create other great leaders in your organization and, therefore, elevate the capacity of your organization to greatness.

Our leadership team meets every Tuesday morning at 8:30 for ninety minutes, no RSVP required. We assume that if you don't show up, you're dead and that we will have to close the office down at the end of the week for your funeral!

Like must-see TV, this is a must-go-to meeting. It is almost like our weekly board of directors meeting, where we discuss some of the most important decisions for the direction of the company. We try to keep it strategic and not tactical, but we do catch up on the news of the week. Most of all, this weekly meeting is my opportunity to lead my team of leaders face-to-face. Then these leaders have their own meetings once a week with people they themselves supervise.

Now more than ever, it's important to surround yourself with the right people and encourage emotional fitness. Let me talk a little bit about what I mean by that.

One of the mistakes I made early on is I focused almost exclusively on what my unique ability was, which was working on the intellectual property of my business, building up the firm, bringing in the business, etc. At the time I thought that if I focused on my abilities alone, that would be good enough. But somehow it turned out it wasn't. Because the organization did not take off until I became a coach to my leaders and a coach to my team. In the end an entrepreneur is just another member of the team.

Great leaders create great followers, but great leaders also create other great leaders.

Part of being a strategic figure is encouraging your team to understand the values and visions you have for your company. If you know emotional fitness helps you, as a leader, make sound decisions, you can be certain that it's probably something you should also encourage in your leaders and, therefore, in your soldiers too.

The pandemic was a magnifying glass, displaying a zoomed-in view of people's true endurance and capabilities. Emotionally fit entrepreneurs who wanted to create a better future used the pandemic to propel and turbocharge their businesses and their lives. They worked hard to be these great leaders and foster the right culture and beliefs in their folks to make it through the hurdles and past the obstacles toward success. The folks who didn't use the pandemic as an excuse to fail perform poorly or give up.

As Vince Lombardi once said, "Perfection is not attainable, but if we chase perfection, we can catch excellence." We want to be emotionally fit, hire the right people, and support the best leaders so that we catch those glimpses of perfection and breathe them into our own lives and businesses.

FIRE MORE CLIENTS THAN FIRE YOU

When I started my business, I was reviewing my weekly schedule one day when I noticed that all I was routinely scheduling was my lunch break and the occasional haircut. That was the extent of my robust calendar. I had absolutely nobody to see. So if I could have gotten an appointment with the chair next to me, I would have scheduled the appointment and penciled that into my robust calendar too. I was that desperate for appointments.

That's the first trap of becoming an entrepreneur: scarcity. Not having enough clients or business or slots filled. This drives you to meet with anyone who'll agree to meet with you. When you're starting out, often, your business is operating in survival mode, so, like a starving man, you take whatever you can get. You grab a saltine.

The second trap of an entrepreneur is the ego trap. It's the "I can help everybody in the world. There isn't a soul around I cannot help."

As a result of this mindset, you start to bring in and attract clients who consume a disproportionate share of your time for the effort that they're truly worth.

But more importantly your team follows suit in your footsteps, and soon, they are draining their time and resources, too, on these clients who seem an ill, if desperate, fit for your company. Clients who won't respect your values, your rules, your processes and sometimes clients who don't respect or value your worth. Soon, your employees start to pick up on these signals, and often they, too, start to lose respect for you. Whether they voice it out loud or not, they start to wonder, "Why are we putting up with this nonsense from this client who just won't follow the rules and doesn't really seem as committed to the process as we are? We've got other great clients." Just like choosing a significant other who's an unemployed serial cheater, what could possibly be the rationale behind taking on a client who's a rude jerk with no money?

The first thing you've got to do as an entrepreneur is let go of your ego and realize you can't be the savior for everybody. What this does is release you and your team from chasing the riffraff that aren't worth your time or efforts.

It's only then that epiphany will strike, and you'll realize that who you're really looking for in most clients is yourself. Your very best clients are going to be the clients who are most like you. What does that mean? Say, for example, if you're loyal, your clients, too, will tend to be loyal. If you're hardworking, they, too, will tend to be hardworking. If you appreciate their knowledge, they will appreciate yours. If you're a big thinker, they most likely will be too. If you're looking for a transformational relationship, they're most probably looking for a transformational relationship too. To some extent, this reinforces theories about the universe we often hear: you will attract the energy you put out there. The same is true here. You will attract and will want to work with the people who are most aligned to your own values and beliefs.

As a starting point, I always encourage entrepreneurs to figure out what their nonnegotiables and core values are. That should be the starting point. What are the components that you're absolutely not willing to compromise on whatsoever? Exceptional service? An environmental-friendly product?

I'll give you a few examples of my own nonnegotiables. Say, we're working on a project, one of my nonnegotiables is to always beat the client to communication.

For instance, if you're relying on a third party to get back to you and you still haven't gotten what you need from them, it's up to you to call the client and say, "Hey, listen. It's Jane. I thought I'd have an

The first thing you've got to do as an entrepreneur is let go of your ego and realize you can't be the savior for everybody.

answer for you about XYZ by today. I spoke to the other party this morning, but they said they probably won't have an answer until Tuesday. I'll give you a call Tuesday afternoon to touch base."

That's much better than scrambling at eleven o'clock Sunday night trying to find answers when the client reaches out demanding to know why they've been getting the silent treatment. At that point you're already operating in a loss from my perspective.

The other nonnegotiable for me is treating clients like they're truly special and cared for. I'm sure we can all think of instances where we've called a business and been placed on hold for forty-five minutes only to be disconnected. Or come across someone who is rude as heck.

Or maybe you remember a time when you called about an issue and the customer care representative acted like you *were* the issue.

When we answer the phone, we talk to clients like we have all day to talk to only them. I want them to feel like their call is the one we've been waiting for all day. For my company personally, these are a few of our nonnegotiables—the types of services and actions we absolutely will not compromise on.

Once you identify your nonnegotiables, the other component to think through is what are the core values of your company? For ideas, keep reading—I'll share examples of my company's core values in a later chapter. Feel free to steal some if you'd like. But once you know what your nonnegotiables and core values are, you've essentially created a strong baseline you can use to start attracting people (whether clients or employees) whose values are in line with yours.

SPECIALIZE AND SET EXPECTATIONS

When I was a kid, there were just three main television stations. That meant that the programs on these stations were sort of dumbed down to appeal to a mass audience. Now there are almost no television shows or news outlets that are generic to appeal to everybody. They all cater to a very specific demographic or niche. There are networks that appeal only to women, only to Black people, only to conservatives, only to children, etc.

Entrepreneurs need to work in the same way. Focus your efforts on a specific demographic, a certain group, a certain range of ages, a certain gender. Don't be so broad and try to cater to the world—get specific! Now that doesn't mean you shouldn't cast a wide net, but know that you will attain the best results if you reach out to people who have a natural proclivity to appreciating or seeking your services.

Also, once you garner the interest of a client, make it clear up front what the expectations are for working with your company. Then it's up to them whether they still feel confident abiding by those expectations enough to opt in or opt out. That's important because a fast "no" is much better than a slow one. The mistake we entrepreneurs sometimes make is carrying clients for weeks, months, and sometimes even for years who don't quite fit into our mold. If we shared up front how we work, they would have never hired us or cost us time, money, effort, energy, anxiety, or agita.

With new clients, share your value proposition. For instance, let's say that part of the agreement to working together is that when a client calls you, either you're going to pick up the phone immediately or you're going to call back within an hour unless you're on an airplane or underwater or something. They'll come to expect a quick response, but you're also going to expect the same from them. This is your mutual agreement on how you'll work together. If the client says, "I'll call you whenever I want. You work for me," then that person doesn't have respect for the way you work. That's when the juice is just not worth the squeeze.

Do you want your staff to be treated rudely by people who think the world owes them a living? Cut these clients loose. They are not worth your time, your efforts, or your skill. It might sound hard, even counterintuitive, to let business—any kind of business—slip through your fingers like sand. But let me assure you that when you cut your losses, you will free up your time and your staff's time. You must decide who you want to be a hero for. For me it is my team, entrepreneurs, and entrepreneurial-thinking people. By letting unsuitable business go, you'll become a hero in the eyes of your staff because you won't allow anybody to treat them in a way that doesn't match your core values. As a result, they'll gain respect and perhaps even a sense of loyalty toward you and the company.

Now let's back up a bit. Because as a general rule, the customer is always right, if the client wants things done a certain way, you should try to accommodate them. But sometimes the team is even more important than a single client, and you must protect your team first and treat them with the same care and concern, if not more, as you would your clients. Because at the end of the day, that team is what's going to help you hold up the fort. It's they who are going to help you retain clients, win new ones, and keep your business running and doors open.

That doesn't mean you need to operate like that Soup Nazi from *Seinfeld*. For those of you who aren't familiar with the show, there's an episode where an employee in a restaurant is referred to as a Soup Nazi. All customers want is a bowl of soup, but if you don't follow the Soup Nazi's rules, he won't give you any. Don't go that far. Don't be a Soup Nazi. I do suggest, however, that you have a set of standards that aren't detrimental to your clients but still protect you and your team so that when you bring in a dollar of revenue, it won't cost $10 of chaos and pain and expense. That's simply just not worth it.

Let's talk now about how to make sure your business is aimed at the right people.

DESIGN YOUR BUSINESS

Building on our earlier point, just like television caters programming and channels to a specific audience, you, too, must design your business around a specific target group. Get clear on who your business is for and how it will make their lives better, easier, happier. One of the great ironies in our business is that just like many of the employees that got you where you are do not have the skill sets to get you where you're going, many of the great clients that got your business where it is will not be the people that take you where you're destined to go.

How do I know this? Through years in the industry helping entrepreneurs and through my own experiences. One of the things we've tried to do at our company is have it go both ways—to great pain. We've continued to service clients that were with us for many, many years because of their loyalty, which we felt needed to be reciprocated, even if from a business standpoint, it was not the best decision. If I were a ruthless businessman, I would have set them loose because they were not the right fit for our business, but I am also loyal. It's a trade-off that fits our core values.

When it comes to attracting business, ask yourself, do you want customers, or do you want clients? A customer is a transactional relationship that you could lose at any time, for any reason. A client is a transformational relationship with somebody who wants to be in a relationship with you, who wants to work with you. If you're working with a transactional client, ask yourself this: why are you pouring your heart and soul into somebody who does not value the experience with you?

Personally, while I find the work with transactional customers to be almost joyless, I find the transformational relationships, which are overwhelmingly most of our clients, an honor and a privilege to be able to serve. The key is that they value what we do, and that's what makes our work all the more fulfilling and successful.

At our company, we work to have transformational initiatives where both parties are emotionally and physically committed to obtaining the best results. Our clients are basically there telling us that they want us to be a consigliere and a teammate and a tour guide. And that's integral. Because think of it this way: if your client is looking for a five-star meal and you own a McDonald's or Pizza Hut, you're probably not going to be the restaurant that best caters to their tastes. On the other hand, if you have a five-star restaurant with gourmet ingredients and seven-course meals but they just want to get out for half an hour and have a slice of pizza and a Diet Coke, again, they're not going to come to you. Or if they do, they won't be happy.

It's like dating someone who wants something completely different from you out of your relationship. You're saying, "Let's get married," and they're saying, "Let's go out for coffee every couple of months." Not saying they shouldn't get their requested coffee date. They most certainly should but probably not with you. What does coffee and marriage have anything to do with business, Mark, you might ask? All I'm trying to say and prove is that some people in life simply won't deserve you. Not the experience of being with you and sometimes not the experience of working with you. When you create something that you think is special and somebody does not see the value in what you do, why should they deserve the pleasure of experiencing it? Do you want to pour your heart and soul into something that somebody can simply choose to take or chuck aside at their whim? Or do you want someone who will appreciate what you have, see the value in it, and be excited by it?

By choosing to do business with just about anyone, your team ends up taking a beating. They don't succeed because you've got the wrong clientele. It's like me wanting you to win the Kentucky Derby, but instead of a thoroughbred, I hand you a mule. Why isn't this mule winning the Kentucky Derby? Because it's a mule! This takes us to my next point; see who's working and see who's not. And look very carefully.

WEED OUT WHAT DOESN'T WORK

Businesses need a repeatable and reliable process that helps them determine which clients are right for them and which ones are not. You need to be transparent with potential clients and up front about what it's like to work with you.

We have a process that allows us to weed out clients who wouldn't work well with us so that when I have that second meeting with them and it's time to decide whether we're going to move into a relationship or not, they've had several chances to expose who they really are. In the end we choose to align ourselves in relationships with clients who believe that their future is always bigger than their past. They are big dreamers and big thinkers. They improve the lives of everyone they touch. What's the opposite of that? Somebody who comes from scarcity, someone who thinks nothing good or new can happen. If you've got folks with too much baggage who are not open-minded, unfortunately, you can't help them. That just means we are not the right firm for them.

Your approach depends on how you conduct your sales. You don't want to be like those "free vacation weekends" at a timeshare where you end up spending most of your time enduring high-pressure sales tactics. I think some businesses hide the ball as blatantly as those timeshare salespeople. They may pull a bait and switch on you. They may not be clear on who they are. All they're focused on is landing the business, regardless of whether or not the client is a good fit for them and vice versa.

If you're in business and you believe that you're creating value for people, you should be transparent and up front with them. Then if they're not the right fit, either they would self-select out of your service or you could help get them to the right person so you don't spend weeks, days, months, years with the wrong client.

Remember this because it's worth reiterating: doing business with the wrong people will always only strain your organization, making working there less fun and rewarding. But when you have the right clients, the same work becomes exhilarating and fun. Time flies when the work is purposeful and you're making a difference in people's lives. With the wrong people, it's drudgery, it's exhausting, and it's painful.

This brings us to another important question, especially if you're already in the thick of things with your business: what happens if you discover you've taken on the wrong client? In other words, how do you fire a client? Well, ultimately, our approach is the same as it has been with employees whom we determine are no longer a good fit for the company. First, you put the onus on them, giving them a chance to discover on their own that your company may not be the place for them. Be transparent and point out that you see they're not happy or that they're too talented or too smart to spend the next ten, fifteen, or twenty years in a relationship that doesn't work.

If there are blatant issues, it's important you address them in a direct yet sensible way. Whatever the issue, try to talk them through why you both might be a misfit for the other. You could say something like "Every day the people in our organization try their best to make you happy." Then give them some examples, maybe two or three, of some things you've done to help make their lives better. Then point out where they didn't hold up their end of the bargain, such as yelling at one of your employees or using improper language. You can close out with a statement like "For the past three years, we've done everything we can to satisfy you, but it doesn't seem as though we are succeeding. We must be missing the mark. We're confident there's probably another firm out there that's a better fit for you."

Whatever you do, don't get confrontational. Don't say, "Here's your file. Let me hit you over the back of the head on the way out the door." Handle it in a sophisticated manner. You don't need retribution or to exchange cross words. You just need them gone. Why not do it in a respectful way that maintains the integrity of your company and its reputation?

The truth is, a lot of companies out there are happy to take on any business, right? One person's crumb is another person's steak.

Over time you will find that you'll need to weed out fewer and fewer clients. Eventually you'll begin to attract and retain clients who are the right fit from the get-go.

HUBRIS IS THE RUINATION OF HABIT

Bill Gates said that early in his career, he overvalued intelligence when he should have put more weight into *emotional* intelligence skills, like self-awareness. In my thirty-five years of hiring and working with people, I have found that self-awareness can help you avoid hubris, which is the ruination of all habit.

It's hubris that leads some people to believe that what's happening now will happen forever. For instance, the stock bull run that started in 2010 can make people who have only been investing for the past decade or so act with hubris. They haven't seen market cycles that wipe out portfolios like in the '80s, '90s, and 2000s, so they think the stock market only goes one way: straight up. Maybe they think that real estate goes straight up, too, and that nobody dies or becomes disabled. They believe there's no interruption in income because they haven't experienced it before. There'll be no unexpected or unintended things happening in life, so they fail to prepare for such events. (Conversely, people who have been burned in investments may deny themselves the ability to put money at risk because, based on their experience, they think investments only lose money.)

Often, we tend to assume that people who file for bankruptcy, lose their house, or can't afford to send their kids to college must have gotten sick or lost a job when in reality, more often than not, it's hubris that got in their way. Maybe they made ungodly amounts of money, but they had the wrong belief systems around finances. In fact, one of my favorite expressions is, "It's all BS ... It's all belief systems."

Belief systems are absolutely crucial. One of the things I've become acutely aware of over the last decade is that when people don't have the right belief systems around money, they'll keep relying and falling back on the same bad habits, even when you help them succeed. Say, a client is making $300,000 a year but has too much debt and not enough investments. They come to us, and we're able to help them double their income. Now they're making $600,000, and that should be phenomenal and fix everything. Right? Wrong. Someone with the wrong belief systems around money will manage to somehow take the benefit of a doubled income and end up doubling their problems too. Maybe even tripling or quadrupling them.

Many of the mistakes that people make in business and in life are based on the arrogance that hubris brings. They get blindsided because they believe that bad things happen only to other people. They believe their spouse will never lose a job or a child will never get sick. That the roof's not going to blow off in a storm, leading to tens of thousands of dollars in unexpected expenses. Unfortunately, life happens, and it can happen to anyone. Yes, even you. That's where having the right financial belief system can help.

YOUR FINANCIAL BELIEF SYSTEM

Even the most affluent people can have hidden land mines in their lives that they have not prepared for. When we work with these clients, we help them dig out the land mines and start making wise choices. For instance, some people come to us with a lot of credit card debt—tens of thousands, even hundreds of thousands, of dollars' worth of debt. So we put together a plan that helps them pay off the debt, but then, unfortunately, a year or two later, some of them are right back to where they'd started, maybe even worse off than before.

Digging them out of debt didn't help because although our tactics to help them better manage their money changed, their belief systems remained the same. It's like picking someone up at the Betty Ford Clinic with a fifth of scotch or a bottle of vodka. They've cleared their credit cards, but they didn't set up the right belief systems around money. So they don't have the tools or resources in place to avoid making the same bad mistake again.

For some, it's too hard to control the impulse to fall back on bad habits. To some extent, they become your default setting. I understand this all too well because I've had a lifelong food addiction. I celebrated with food, and I comforted myself with food, so I have to work very hard to make sure my relationship with food remains healthy by having the right belief systems around it in place. The same goes for money. Maybe you can't afford the house your sister got so you shouldn't try to keep up with the Joneses. That's hubris getting in your way.

You need to learn to accept and anticipate deferred gratification. One of the things I say to my NFL clients, whose careers last an average of three and a half years, is, "Do you want to be king for a few years or prince for a lifetime?" Sometimes players think that either their income will go on forever or they're not going to live very long. So their belief systems prevent them from thinking long term about money. Then when they damage their knee or age out and retire and they're no longer making millions of dollars a year, it's like they threw this big party that's now come to an abrupt end.

A client of mine who was a doctor had a gambling issue. By the time he was sixty-five, he had gone through every dime to his name. At the same time, his wife was under the impression that they were ready to retire. I had to sit her down and gently explain that they had no money left. Meanwhile, he was giving $80,000 to the bookies who'd just taken $40,000 of his money, thinking they had some insider knowledge and his luck was about to change. He was a very smart doctor, but he lost everything because of his flawed financial belief systems. When it comes to money, you need to think into the future. So let's talk about that.

YOUR MONEY'S SUSTAINABILITY

You need to think about the long-term sustainability of your money. Saving and building wealth is not like those old-school Christmas clubs, where you stash money away every week just so you can spend it all on Christmas presents at the end of the year. Rather, it's about building long-term wealth where your money does the work. This is an important concept to remember: here, we're not talking about putting people to work; we're talking about putting money to work. But that's a hard concept for some people to understand.

I want you to have a great life, but the one thing we all know by now is that tomorrow is not promised to anyone. That's why I encourage you to take a percentage of your money and put it away. Put it where, you might wonder? And my answer is anywhere! Now by making that statement, I'm not saying that I don't care that you put it in the right place. However, it's far more important that you take the time to put it away, out of sight, than focusing on exactly where you put it. That can come next. Have a long-term commitment to investment. This includes investing in your business, too, not just stocks, bonds, money market funds, and insurance. Your money should be diversified.

Years ago I worked with two young executives at a major investment bank who each owned about $10 million of stock in their company. That was most of their net worth at the time, and they both thought that the company's stock was going to do nothing but go up. Young executive number one believed his stock would increase two- or threefold, making it worth upward of $30 million. I suggested that he take out half and invest it elsewhere, just in case the stock didn't perform or failed altogether. That way he'd help protect his portfolio. But he figured I didn't know what I was talking about, and so he ignored my advice and kept all his money in his company's stock.

> *Saving and building wealth is not like those old-school Christmas clubs, where you stash money away every week just so you can spend it all on Christmas presents at the end of the year.*

Young executive number two reluctantly sold half his company stock and put it into other investments. A few years later, the company went out of business and its stock was suddenly worth zero dollars.

It was hubris to say "Hey, our company's value is only going straight up, and putting everything in that company stock is the way to go!"

Now every time I see exec number one, he curses at me and says, "I should have listened to you." Exec number two hugs me. He's also retired in his fifties while the other guy is still grinding away.

In real estate markets, clients believe that if buying one place is great, then buying fifteen places must be fifteen times as great. But then, suddenly, there's some downturn or interruption in the market, and they don't have enough liquidity. Maybe a big tenant moves out and their rent slows down or maybe some big economic event interrupts rent collection, and suddenly, all fifteen properties go bankrupt. They could have easily withstood the downturn in the real estate market had they pursued just two or three properties. Then they could accumulate that third or fourth or fifth property at pennies on the dollar at a more opportune time. Unfortunately, people often fall prey to what I call the entrepreneurial God complex.

THE ENTREPRENEURIAL GOD COMPLEX

Sometimes hubris leads entrepreneurs to acquire a God complex. This is where they begin to believe they can continue their success indefinitely. Often, they're smart and perhaps lucky, and they've found a niche where they can be an expert. They build a company and earn amazing cash flow and wealth—and then they think they can do that endlessly in every vertical. They've always bet on themselves and won, so why not, right? But even the best-laid plans can go south, as we all know.

Think of it this way too. When you're just starting out as an entrepreneur, you have nothing to lose, so you can double, triple, and quadruple down to go all in. As you progress in life, however, you'll have responsibilities and more assets to your name that need protecting, and so you need to make sure you're being thoughtful with how you employ your capital; otherwise, you could face some grave losses and, in a worst-case scenario, wipe away decades of hard work.

Now that I'm in my fifties, I check with my lawyers, accountants, regulators, and compliance people before I make a big decision. (Remember, even the smartest folks need somebody to help them navigate the right decisions.)

I remember when my fiancée had a great business idea. The first thing I told her was we need to sit down with her attorney to protect ourselves from a lawsuit that could put everything we have at risk. That's a big difference from the mindset I would have at twenty-two. Likely, back then my response would have been "Screw it. What are they going to sue me for? They can take my blow-up mattress!"

I'm not saying once you've made some money that you have to hunker down and avoid risk. Let the entrepreneur be the entrepreneur. Let that entrepreneurial spirit loose. But just do it in a more thoughtful way because you shouldn't remain an open target to risks and mistakes when you have more to protect.

Hubris often gets in the way when someone has sunken a lot of money into a project. Let's say you bought a stock at $108 a share, and now it's worth only $52 per share. Most people would probably insist on holding on to the stock until its value rises back up to $108. I'll intervene and explain that although I can't do anything to change how much they bought the stock at, the word on the street is that the value is going to drop further. I'll advise people to sell and buy something else that's going up, but often people will resist. The same applies when someone has put $2 million into a company division that's not working. Instead of admitting that it has a bad business model, they borrow yet another $2 million to sink further into this bad vehicle. Fortunately, there is a way to avoid the foibles of hubris and the God complex.

SEEK OUTSIDE COUNSEL AND FIND YOUR DHARMA

As I mentioned, sometimes because of hubris, it's tough to see things clearly when you're emotionally involved. I call this emotion the six-hundred-pound spoon. Say, for instance, there are a saucer and a spoon on the table. Two friends are drinking coffee. One sees the spoon as a utensil. The other has a completely different history with and phobia of spoons: he tripped over one and broke his big toe; he was poked in the eye with one when he was little and ended up at the doctor's. Another time, his sibling poked a spoon end up his nose and made him bleed. That spoon to the first person is nothing more than a piece of metal weighing a few measly ounces that facilitates eating. But to the second person, it's all of a sudden this daunting, ominous piece of weaponry that can cause damage.

Sometimes even the smallest, most innocuous things seem impossibly big and daunting to us when emotions are involved or history or perception is involved.

You can take the example of Superman here too. Usually, he's uncharacteristically strong, but a small piece of kryptonite can paralyze him. If anyone else were to take that same piece of kryptonite, they could pick it up and toss it over their shoulder like it's nothing more than a piece of rubble. But for Superman, that kryptonite could prove to be his very demise.

What I mean by either of those examples is that when we are too close or too emotionally involved, it becomes tough to see the forest for the trees.

Worse, when you're a head honcho and believe something to be the six-hundred-pound spoon, few around you will have the courage to tell you otherwise because, like many successful entrepreneurs, you've surrounded yourself with "yes" people. You're their meal ticket, so they don't want to upset the golden goose by speaking the truth.

At the same time, you certainly don't want to surround yourself with negative people either. Instead, you need people whom you can trust to tell you the truth every time.

When you become too successful, you're at risk of becoming the emperor in "The Emperor's New Clothes." You have a harder time finding out what's really going on in your organization because you grow isolated from the worker bees. As the boss, you're busy steering the ship, so to say, versus down in the planks doing the work.

The other caveat to success is that you start to develop a "Midas touch" because you're constantly around people who are telling you how great and incredible you are—because you have money.

But as a leader, I appreciate critical feedback. I will never punish anybody, even the most junior person in the organization, for constructive discourse or open dialogue. Because that helps me be a better leader and lead a better organization. I prize relationships where I can candidly ask someone, "Hey, was I wrong on this? Was I thinking about this correctly?"

However, sometimes I find that being in power can land you in a quagmire of sorts because fewer people are willing to criticize you or be open with you.

As an entrepreneur, you don't want a bunch of yes-men around you. You need someone—an old man, a janitor, a little kid, the front desk receptionist—to say "Hey, emperor, you have no clothes!"

Sure, you don't want to crush your entrepreneurial genius, but at the same time, you also want to make sure that trusted people can help entrepreneurs beta test or fact-check their thoughts and ideas. I'm generally not swayed easily, but there is a group of people I trust. I value their opinions. But I always keep my own counsel. That is, when I make a bad decision, I believe it's on me. I'm a big boy, and I take responsibility for my decisions.

Unfortunately, hubris keeps too many people from seeking outside counsel or maintaining a good support system around them. It's that God complex again, rearing its big ugly head. But because of this complex, many people wind up making an awful lot of mistakes because there are no checks and balances. Those are the people who end up filing for bankruptcy or, God forbid, committing suicide, when just years earlier, they were worth hundreds of millions of dollars. Why does that happen? Again, thanks to hubris and BS— belief systems around money.

When you work with people who are afraid of the six-hundred-pound spoon, you have one of two options: One, you tell them the truth: that the spoon doesn't weigh six hundred pounds. It weighs a couple of ounces, and you're happy to pass it to them. The second thing you can do is surround them with people who can help them deal with whatever issue is making that spoon appear insurmountable to them, helping them focus on their strengths instead of the weaknesses the spoon stirs up (pun intended) inside them.

Spoons aside, I'd say it's also important to find your dharma. The word "dharma" is a bit hard to define. It's like the definition of pornography given in the 1964 Supreme Court case about obscenity:

I know it when I see it. The right dharma fits like a glove; it's the place you're meant to be. For instance, my dharma is that I'm always in my best place when I'm serving others. I could serve people all day, every day. In fact, I've probably done it for sixteen or eighteen hours a day for thirty-five years because it just never tends to seem like work. Serving is something I view as a privilege and an honor, whereas others might prefer to work by themselves in creative pursuits without much interaction with other people at all. That's their dharma. You'll know your dharma when you have it. Because in that moment, it'll feel like you're exactly where you should be.

It's like dating. When I met Lisa DeMayo, I came home from my first date and asked my son to be my best man. I knew I was going to marry her. (By the way, thank God she knew it too!)

If I'm doing something that is the right thing in my dharma, I'll have unlimited energy, passion, and excitement for it. That's when you see everything click into place in your life. That's when you know the world has you right where you should be.

THE PREPARED AND NIMBLE WILL SURVIVE

———

When most people think of a great artist, a great athlete, a great ballerina—any great performer—they mistakenly attribute or chalk up these people's talents to natural ability. Of course, there's no doubt that to some extent, these performers have some inherent gift. But for the most part, it's really preparation and a repeatable process honed over time and a grave commitment to their craft for years, sometimes decades, that propels them to success. It boils down to preparation.

When I was a student at Indiana University, Bob Knight was our winning coach, but he was also a controversial coach. Yet nobody questioned his methods because he won national championships for the team.

What made him controversial? He was accused of choking his players, throwing a chair across the floor during a game, punching out some fans, and also knocking the lights out of a referee. And yet this man was deemed great. The greatest basketball coach, in my opinion, that America has ever had.

The one thing Knight always coached his team to never do was to never call a time-out toward the end of a very close game. He believed the game was won during painstaking practices that prepared his team physically and psychologically for those last two minutes on the court. He had already coached his team for what could happen in those crucial two minutes, so he figured, why give the other coach a chance to prepare the opposing players?

His team wasn't necessarily better or more athletic than any other team, and yet they were winning national championships. They weren't the best players. But thanks to a unified strategy and outlook, they were the best *team*. What makes the best team?

THE RIGHT PLAYERS MAKE THE BEST TEAM

If you're an entrepreneur, you want to make sure you have the best players on your team. But it's equally as important for those teammates to know their roles and stay in their lanes. Sometimes you see business teams with lots of talent, but either they have too many people with similar skills, or they have people who refuse to stick to their own roles. Either scenario could end up costing you the game.

Think of it this way: You could have the best quarterback in the league, but if the wide receiver can't catch the ball, it doesn't matter how good the quarterback is. I see this type of analogy play out repeatedly at company after company. So while preparedness is the number one priority, the number two concern, as we've mentioned previously and is worth reiterating, is getting the right people in the right seats to put a complete, robust team in place.

I love sports (clearly), so I like to explain this statement best using a basketball metaphor: You can't get on the fast break or on offense if you don't have the ball. But the only way to get the ball is if someone on the team is willing to rebound it. Yet rebounding is sometimes not a glamorous job. Without it, though, you can't win. So if you have a bunch of prima donnas who can't or won't rebound, you're not going to win too many games because you'll never get the ball.

For those of you who aren't sports afficionados and want a more simplistic way to understand, you could think of it like the old saying, "An amateur practices until he gets it right; a professional practices until he can't get it wrong."

So first and foremost, you need a team of professionals. Sometimes, when you have new, talented people, they're still trying to get it just right, but what you really need for them to do is to make sure that they can't get it wrong.

They also need a commitment level of "Hell yeah." It's like that old analogy about breakfast: When you're having bacon and eggs, the chicken is involved, but the pig is committed. At the risk of sounding cheesy and odd, I'll say you want all pigs in your organization. I want everybody in my organization to be a pig so that they are fully committed.

Too often, however, entrepreneurs get so caught up in the sale of the product and service to the customer they forget the commitment level of their pigs—whether that's them themselves or their employees. Their core values must hold the standard to their partners and employees or they will be mediocre at best and uncommitted at worst. Once you're committed, hang on and hang on tight. Because the world is like a carousel where change is the only constant.

THE NIMBLE ARE OPEN-MINDED TO CHANGE

At the turn of the twentieth century, the world was changing every couple of decades or so. Then about thirty-five years ago, when I first went into business, it seemed that business was changing every five to seven years. Now there are disruptions in the market happening at lightning speed. Sometimes change happens not in years but in months. So not only do you need to continue to be innovative to remain in competition, but you must also build a company that's nimble so you can avoid being left behind—or going as extinct as the dinosaurs. When you're nimble and open to change, you're ensuring that anytime the world or the country or your industry gets disrupted, you're at the ready to ride the wave and not be swept under the tide.

Of course, not everyone thinks this way. Many people fail to prepare for the changes the future might bring. For instance, a client may inherit money from their parents or grandparents, who insist that the heir invests it in certain stocks. Unfortunately, by the time they pass, it's been decades since the will was written, and now the world has changed drastically. So drastically that most of the companies they wanted their heir to invest in no longer even exist, having gone out of business years earlier. The heir, therefore, is left at an unfortunate crossroads because, of course, they can't invest their money in companies that no longer exist.

These types of scenarios led me to a harsh realization: if the largest companies in the world were disappearing at such a rapid rate, no doubt the medium- and smaller-sized companies, too, were facing a similar, if not swifter, demise.

So when I talk about and encourage you to be nimble, I mean for you to be nimble so you can *anticipate* what's ahead, not so you can simply *react* to what happens. But that's where most people run into a problem. Because they are reactive when what they need to be is proactive so they are able to anticipate disruptions and perhaps even create a disruption or two themselves. The proactive companies who are focused on anticipation are the ones that continue to flourish for years and even decades into the future.

What makes for a nimble business? To be nimble, the first and foremost attribute you must possess is being open-minded to change. Most people say, "Well, this is how we've always done it." If you're one of them, you're falling prey to what's called groupthink and group culture. This type of culture is the one that insists, "This is the only way we do things." But that's where you need to tweak your mindset and help yourself realize that you must evolve and change.

When I started at Northeast Private Client Group back in 1985, I did virtually everything under the sun that my staff of employees do now—except I did it single-handedly. I was always taking on multiple tasks and responsibilities, hefting the burden of it all on my shoulders alone. Now a CEO, I have very few job descriptions. I

When you're nimble and open to change, you're ensuring that anytime the world or the country or your industry gets disrupted, you're at the ready to ride the wave and not be swept under the tide.

shake hands and kiss babies. I build relationships to close deals. I work on the intellectual property of the firm. All the high-level tasks that don't involve the down-in-the-weeds involvement I was once known to be engaged in. In other words, I evolved as the company changed. In the same way, the world requires you to evolve as a successful entrepreneur; it also requires you to innovate.

GOOD LEADERS INNOVATE

It's my job every year to try to innovate at least three new, big ideas or three new, big strategies that we can introduce to the rest of our team. I've still got to make sure I'm bringing in the money and closing deals, but I also need to make our company viable five years from now, ten years from now, or twenty years from now by continuing to come up with big ideas, three innovations every year at a time.

It's like hockey when the great Wayne Gretzky said he doesn't skate where the puck is but where it's going to go. Like Gretzky, I need to be able to have an organization that's nimble. I need to be able to envision where we are going to go and traverse a path toward that trajectory for the entire company. Every year my goal is to put last year's company out of business. I want our current company to seem antiquated and a relic of the past.

It's clear to me that change is often good for entrepreneurs, even when it doesn't look like it. While the pandemic has had costs—in people's lives, health, and freedom—it's been an opportunity for the nimble to flourish. Remember, as we said earlier, this pandemic has served as a magnifying glass, bringing into deeper focus who each of us really are. The nimble and strong companies figured out a way to reinvent themselves and come back bigger, better, and stronger than before. But mediocre companies used the pandemic as an excuse for their failures.

What it all boils down to is the way you think. My high school principal used to say there are three types of people in the world: people who make things happen, people who wait for things to happen, and people who say, "What happened?"

I'm not suggesting at all that you have the clairvoyance or powers of predictability that Nostradamus did to see into the future and make things happen accordingly. No. But an entrepreneur does need to have a belief system that reinforces that the future will unfold in direct correlation to the efforts and hard work they're willing to put in. Not everybody has the will to succeed or the strength to prepare and innovate. Rather, the question is, do you have the will to *prepare* for success?

Great fortunes were wiped out during this pandemic, and great fortunes were built. Which side of the coin do you want to be?

And then there's this other thing about being nimble …

YOU CAN'T BE NIMBLE WITH TOO MUCH DEBT

If you want to stay nimble, you cannot layer on too much debt because that, by definition, means your company is no longer nimble. When you have cash on hand and aren't paralyzed by the burden of debt and having to pay back creditors, you can use liquidity to make changes, to evolve, move, and be light on your feet. But debt can be like shackles, impeding your movements.

There's great pressure in this country to spend more than you make. People want the best of the best: the best decor for their lobby, the best coffee bar for clients, the best technology, the best LED TVs for their waiting areas. It's gotten to the point that people overburden their companies with debt, spending frivolously on things that perhaps they really don't need in the moment or could do without initially, at least. When they overburden themselves and there's an unexpected disruption in the industry or a hiccup of some sort in the business, suddenly, they realize they don't have the financial wherewithal to sustain themselves. The next thing you know, their whole empire comes crashing down around them.

I see this in the real estate business all the time. When the real estate market gets hot, people may set out to buy just one property. They then decide that two properties would be better than one. But if two's good, well … four is even better, right? They go around grabbing opportunities like hotcakes thinking only up and never down, falling prey to the God complex. Then when there's a disruption in the marketplace and they don't have enough capital to withstand it, they wind up bankrupt.

There is nothing wrong with a budgeted life. But these days, spending habits tend to align with perfection rather than with reality. What you end up seeing is folks who live above their means, sometimes way above their means. As long as there's no disruption in their cash flow, everything seems to work out fine. But once there's disruption, it's game over, and all comes tumbling down. Bob Ball, the inventor and creator of The Living Balance Sheet®, taught us this.[3] He created the term "financial freedom," which means the financial buckets are filled, turning the word "budgeting" into a positive word rather than a dirty one.

---

3   The Living Balance Sheet® (LBS) and the LBS logo are service marks of The Guardian Life Insurance Company of America (Guardian), New York, NY. © Copyright 2005-2022 Guardian

If you are good at being careful with your expenditures and managing debt and are looking to build wealth, there are a few ways you could go about doing it.

WEALTH CAN BE BUILT WITH PRIVATE EQUITY

If you stay nimble and reduce your debt, you have options with your money. I'm a believer in private equity. That's where wealth can be built.

As the CEO, I work seven days a week. I'm in the trenches every day, and I have been there for three-plus decades, leading and helping to build wealth for my company and my clients. Northeast Private Client Group is my money machine.

But I've also built personal wealth for myself by making investments with my own money in six private equity companies I believe have potential. I have investments in those companies, and I'm usually on the board of directors for them so I can help provide input and steer them, but I don't have the day-to-day responsibility of them. We've hired a very capable board and very capable CEOs and executives, but leading and being in the trenches with these companies the way I am with my own is not my job, nor do I want it to be. Investing in this way has not only created additional wealth and strategic partnerships for me, but it's also allowed me to grow as a CEO by being able to have insight into different companies and other industries.

And it's important that I can also add value to these companies with my experience, my network, or my skill sets.

However, that's not the way many people operate. For instance, I was shadowing one of my sons as he took a finance course in college. He had to participate in an exercise where he received a fictional

$10,000 to invest in any of a hundred fictional companies that were modeled off real ones. Then he was asked to watch videos, and at the end of each one was a short explanation of the value of investing in that particular company. As a student he had to take into consideration the facts and options presented and decide whether to pass on it or invest—and if so, how much to invest.

Now remember, nine out of ten companies don't make it. So although this is still tolerable in a simulation exercise like the one my son was doing, it is a completely different risk and feeling in real life. Plus, this type of investing is not for the faint of heart; this is at the top of the pyramid. This is dream bucket money, but it's money that is not as exciting to me as how I would normally invest. I much prefer to be involved in a company so that I can add value, much like I'm doing in my own company—but without the day-to-day operations (because I already have a job!).

This kind of investing is not the cake. It's the icing on the cake.

I worry, however, about people swinging for the fences in private equity opportunities. When 90 percent of companies fail, these investors are often left in poor financial shape. That's why I believe that when you're investing in private equity, you want to use the Warren Buffett rule: don't invest in anything you don't understand. You could be passing on the next Google or the next Apple, sure. But if I don't understand it, I'm not putting my hard-earned money behind it. And you shouldn't either.

SURROUND YOURSELF WITH PEOPLE WHO SHARE YOUR VISION

If you have an entrepreneurial mindset, you know that you don't grow a business; you grow people. So if you're not hiring people who share your mindset or your core values or all the things that are important to you, what other real purpose do you have as a leader or business owner?

If we're in agreement that we're growing people, why would you surround yourself with people who don't share your vision or people who even go against it? I'm not saying that your employees should have the vision of the founder—there's usually only one visionary in a company, and that should be you. But you need to (and can truly only) grow the people who share your core values and can buy into your vision.

Gino Wickman writes about the EOS, which is a set of concepts and tools designed to help entrepreneurs organize their everyday challenges into cohesive goals. The EOS gave me a system to rate employees against my core values by using the People Analyzer, a report card tool that assesses how well employees and new hires match your company's values. This exercise gave us rocket fuel in our organization because then we had, as Wickman says, "the right people in the right seats." It was amazing how things took off after that.

But to put the right people in those seats, let's rewind a bit and talk about how you can get the right people through your doors to begin with.

GOOD ENOUGH ISN'T GOOD ENOUGH

It's hard to find great talent; not everybody can be a player. I have come to the conclusion that you're better off with fewer people who share your core values than more people who don't.

There are buzzwords and catchphrases that are red flags in my company. One of them is "That employee is good enough." It's like the devil you know versus the devil you don't, and that isn't good. These days there's a human capital shortage, no doubt. And many employers feel you have to be grateful for whomever you can get your hands on. But I disagree.

I believe in the Field of Dreams mantra when it comes to entrepreneurs and entrepreneurship: "If you build it, they will come." If you have the right vision with the right core values and a common purpose that everybody can rally around, people will be attracted to your company. It's the law of attraction. What you put out there is what you attract.

In many ways this law also reminds me of dating. So many people pray and wish that a knight in shining armor or a beautiful princess will just crop up in their lives. But it doesn't work that way. You have to put actionable items in place—"build it"—so that these people will come and so that you'll attract them. If you're a mediocre company with a mediocre vision, you're going to attract mediocre people. Ask yourself: Is my vision clear? Are my core values clear?

Sometimes core values can look similar from company to company or person to person. That doesn't mean they're right or wrong. It just means they're the right values for your vision and your entrepreneurial spirit.

If you have the right vision with the right core values and a common purpose that everybody can rally around, people will be attracted to your company.

In my experience there'll be a group in your company that gets it right away, and they will be all in and all over your values. There'll be a second group that will hang back in the short term to see if the core values are real, if they're truly adopted, or if they're just convenient values that you talk about but don't hold yourself accountable to when times get tough. They'll observe whether you end up defaulting back on old behaviors. You've got to coach both of these groups but in different ways. Let the first group know that you believe in them so that they believe in themselves and aim higher and higher. Coach the second group by letting them know that your core values are nonnegotiable. Sell them on the vision so they see its value.

However, there's also a third group. This group is there for the paycheck. They're also there to cause trouble. You coach this group to self-select themselves out in a dignified way. Unless it's somebody who has stolen from me or has been abusive, I do everything to help people who fall into this last group by opening up my Rolodex of contacts to find a company where I think they could find success. I've introduced employees to companies where their work and core values would make them successful. I've also offered to write powerful, positive yet honest letters of recommendation.

But first, I sit down with them and say, "It's clear that you're not happy here." I point out that they're not comfortable with the direction the company is headed and that we aren't clicking. "So why would you stay here another five, ten, or twenty years when you're unhappy?" I say to them. "Life is too short for that. I want to be able to help you and empower you forward to a place where you can be truly happy, where there's a smile on your face when you arrive at work every day."

Once you have the right people through the doors and put them in the right seats, it's time to talk core values—because these will be the backbone of your business.

OUR SEVEN CORE VALUES

One of the things that we did early on at Northeast Private Client Group was create seven core values that helped me develop clarity around my vision and the type of people I wanted to have in my business. Now there's no right or wrong number of core values. We have seven, but you might have more or not as many. To give you an idea of what ours look like and perhaps provide some inspiration, here are the ones we live by:

1. Create a wow experience. As a key business strategist, critical thinker, and financial advisor to entrepreneurs and entrepreneurial-thinking people, the first thing I want my team to do is create a wow experience for the client. It's a challenge to your organization that's high tech but also high personal touch.

By high tech, I'm acknowledging the obvious—we live in a world driven by gizmos and gadgets and technology. But I find that the more the world moves toward text and email, the more I realize that the magic, at least in our business and most businesses, lies in human touch and human connection. I would much prefer getting on the phone with somebody because it creates a more personal interaction than if we were just voice texting or emailing back and forth with one another.

Ultimately, the aim is to create a client experience where clients say, "Wow, the only place I can get that experience is by working with your company." If they cannot say that and they are able to get that experience anyplace else with one of your competitors, you're just part of a pack. I want to create a unique, remarkable, and, therefore, memorable experience, and that's what I mean by "wow experience."

To do that, you must operate at a level where your company and your relationship stand out as second to none. No matter what your standard is, keep challenging yourself and your people to create even more of an outstanding expectation for that client. It's almost like being a drug dealer—you want them to get addicted to the high of working with your company so much that they can't do without you.

2. Be a dependable team player. If you're going to work in our company, you've got to be a dependable team player and keep any prima donna tendencies in check. Are you somebody who everybody is glad to have in the foxhole with them? Are you there when things get tough or busy? Are you there to help, even if it's not your responsibility? There is no distinction of winners and losers at our firm. Either we all succeed together or we all fail together. It's important that your coworkers be glad you're on the team.

3. Maintain emotional fitness. When you work with people's money or you work in business, there are going to be stressful times when a client is upset and the work level feels inhumane. You may feel like you need a twenty-eight-hour day to get it all done. Just remember, the more stress there is, the calmer you need to be. Be the beacon in the storm, even when your clients are flipping out. They can have emotional breakdowns, but you can't. You must be the steadying force for them.

4. Have great people skills. I'm a big fan of technology, but I think one of the differentiating factors in many businesses is having a human touch. Many think we're in the financial services business offering money management, financial planning, insurance, and retirement planning. But in reality we're in the people business. So we need people who have great people skills, not only with clients but as good communicators with both me and the rest of the team too.

5. Adopt a growth mindset. Either you're growing or you're shrinking, so pick one. People with a growth mindset have a logical process for getting work done so that when there's too much work to do, they prioritize and get the most important work done first.

I want people who help us build this company to also build real wealth or multigenerational wealth for themselves. We're not just trying to preserve and maintain. Rather, we're always reaching for greater heights, and we're always growing.

6. Be confident but humble. I believe that arrogance and hubris are about as ugly as it gets. When you believe you're "all that," the world has a way of reminding you you're not, and then it knocks you down. As I said earlier, sometimes it knocks gently the first time and a little harder the second time. But the third time, it knocks the arrogance right out of you.

At the same time, you must be a master of your business, which means showing the people you work with and your clients that you're confident you can help solve their problems. You need to show clients you can get to a successful result for them but do so in a humble, serving way. Prove that every day you wake up, you feel gratitude toward these people who have trusted you with a part of their lives.

7. Be innovative and abundant. We do not have a scarcity mindset here. We have an abundance mindset. We're not fighting for the same scarce resource. Rather, there are unlimited resources, plenty to go around for everybody.

Any company that is not innovative is at risk to a disrupter in their business. In other words, you might be a DVD in a world of Netflix or a buggy salesman in an automobile world. Be innovative and abundant and surround the people around you with that energy. Because if you've got your team around these values where there's a single purpose, that means everybody is treading on the same path toward the same goal. That's when excitement builds, because when you have people who have a common vision and the same set of core values, each and every action snowballs into something greater. The people in your organization come to a place of purpose, a single-minded purpose, knowing they're making a difference in the lives of the people they touch. They wake up every day saying, "Hey, I don't have a job. I have a purpose."

I value every single person in our organization because everybody's responsible for the culture and the success of the company. Whether you answer the phones or you're a head honcho at the top of the org chart, you are responsible for the company's core values.

It's like that old story about ten thousand starfish washed up on the beach. The tide goes out and the starfish are all going to die. But a man leans over, picks up one starfish, and throws it back into the ocean. His friend says, "What are you doing? There are ten thousand. You'll never be able to get all ten thousand to safety." The man tells him, "True, but at least I made a difference to that one starfish."

At our company, we're going to make a difference to as many starfish as we can. That's an organization that has a calling. That's an unstoppable team. That's something worth getting out of bed for every morning.

CONCLUSION

·················

We've covered a lot of information. As I said, if you were one of my clients, seated in front of me, hoping for someone to take you through becoming the entrepreneur and investor of your dreams, the advice I've shared in this book is some of the key information I'd share with you face-to-face. I know this because repeatedly over tableside conversations throughout the decades, I've imparted this same advice innumerable times to innumerable individuals just like you: employees, aspiring entrepreneurs, entrepreneurs who just needed real advice and a fair assessment on how they could fall out of the hamster wheel and into a race they actually have a chance at winning.

I hope by now you know how to achieve that: how to progress. How to stop living for a paycheck and start living to build wealth for yourselves and multigenerational wealth for your families.

We've talked about what it means to be a great CEO. We talked about running a great company. We talked about nonnegotiables in the form of our seven core values (of course, yours could be different in number and content). Stay true to those values. Let them be the bastion of your company, employees, and clients. This is integral.

Ultimately, as our organization has grown and continues to grow at a rapid pace, those core values empower us to instill what we stand for.

When I was just starting off in 1985, I had only an assistant who I shared with another advisor. It was easy to keep everyone on track. But now that we've blossomed into a team of thirty—and still growing— our core values are what give our sea of an organization clarity and purpose, both for employees and clients. To me, it's important that either of those groups can examine those values to gauge whether or not we would be a good fit for each other.

Lastly, I would say to you that, other than my children, one of my greatest joys in life has been positively influencing and impacting the lives of so many people we've worked with. And I'm talking about not only our customers but also the people who have worked for us. I marvel at the number of lives we've changed, not only from a wealth perspective but also from the perspective that this little innocent idea that niggled its way into my brain back in 1985 has allowed dozens and dozens of kids to attend college. It's allowed people to pay their mortgages. It's allowed people to do some amazing things in the world—because of what we've created.

I said it at the beginning and I'll say it here again at the end: to me, it was never about the money. I never started this company thinking I wanted to make a boatload of cash. I started this company thinking I wanted to be successful. Sure, I thought and hoped we would make money along the way, but my ultimate priority and main goal always was and always will be to make other people's lives better. And I hope that we've done that, and I hope that we continue to do it even better.

Throughout the years, as I went from having a unique ability to attract clients to developing strategies to help them build wealth, our business never reached its full potential until I learned to be a better leader. Until I learned to be a better CEO. That was the magic sauce to our success.

I hope in this book you've learned some of the key tenets to becoming a great leader too. I hope you've learned how to transition from being self-employed to a true entrepreneur. I hope you learned how to be a good investor. And although this might sound like goodbye, I sure hope it isn't. I would love for this to be the impetus, the spark to your success. I hope, one day, to have the chance to continue this conversation with you one-on-one. I hope one day you will be among those in my life whom I impacted for the better.

CONTACT

Mark B. Murphy

Website: www.markbmurphy.com

LinkedIn: www.linkedin.com/in/mark-b-murphy-813b105

Northeast Private Client Group

Website: www.northeastprivate.com/

LinkedIn: www.linkedin.com/company/
northeast-private-client-group

Facebook: www.facebook.com/NortheastPrivateClient/

YouTube: www.youtube.com/channel/
UCq4Ee6_ifUgKBNoDGAR2Gdw

ABOUT THE AUTHOR

〰〰

Mark B. Murphy is the chief executive officer of Northeast Private Client Group, a national financial planning and wealth management firm. He is the author of *The Win-Win Outcome: The Dealmaker's Guide to Buying and Selling Dental Practices* and *Extraordinary Wealth: The Guide to Financial Freedom and an Amazing Life.*

Murphy is a key business strategist and critical thinker who helps entrepreneurs build real wealth and, in most cases, multigenerational wealth. He provides strategic planning and financial engineering to closely held businesses, mid-size companies, celebrities, athletes, hedge fund managers, doctors, dentists, and other high-net-worth individuals. Murphy believes in creating a "wow" experience for his clients; he feels that true financial wealth is developed by a high level of emotional fitness driven by wealth accumulation strategies and a plan that can work under all circumstances.

Murphy has been ranked #1 in New Jersey and #15 in the nation on the Forbes America's Top Financial Security Professionals List for

2022.[4] This honor is a testament of how he has built a remarkable wealth management practice.

ABOUT THE
CONTRIBUTORS

. . . .

ADAM SCHLOSSBERG, CFP®

Adam Schlossberg, CFP® is the president at Northeast Private Client Group. He has his bachelor's of science degree in finance and risk management from the University of Wisconsin–Madison. Adam has expanded his knowledge and skillset further by obtaining his Series 7 and Series 66 licenses. Adam's continued commitment to education ensures that he is current with financial planning news, information, and trends.

Adam is a key business strategist, critical thinker, and financial advisor to entrepreneurs and entrepreneurial thinking people. He takes a personalized approach by developing, implementing, and monitoring financial and business strategies that meet the different needs of each client. He is always willing to challenge conventional wisdom by thinking outside the box when it comes to investing and preserving wealth.

BENJAMIN J. BUSH, CLU

Benjamin J. Bush, CLU is the managing partner at Northeast Private Client Group. Ben's career in financial services began in 2004 in South Florida where he worked with the National Association for the Self Employed (NASE) and the United Group Association (UGA) to provide benefits to small business owners and individuals. Ben worked closely with Private Client Group for ten years before officially joining the team in 2018. He has his bachelor's of science degree from the University of Florida and holds designations as a Chartered Life Underwriter CLU® and Chartered Financial Consultant ChFC® from the American College.

As a key business strategist and critical thinking financial advisor, Ben offers clients tailored, thoughtful, and objective advice so they can pursue their passions, goals, and dreams. His firm work ethic and genuine desire to help have provided him with opportunities to improve the lives of numerous clients throughout all stages of life and their careers.

Registered Representative and Financial Advisor of Park Avenue Securities LLC (PAS). OSJ: 200 BROADHOLLOW ROAD, SUITE 405, MELVILLE NY, 11747, 631-5895400. Securities products and advisory services offered through PAS, member FINRA, SIPC. Financial Representative of The Guardian Life Insurance Company of America® (Guardian), New York, NY. PAS is a wholly owned subsidiary of Guardian. NORTHEAST PRIVATE CLIENT GROUP is not an affiliate or subsidiary of PAS or Guardian. CA Insurance License #0H30562, AR Insurance License #8196746. 2022-140353 Exp. 7/24

DISCLAIMER

Material discussed is meant for general informational purposes only and is not to be construed as tax, legal, or investment advice. Although the information has been gathered from sources believed to be reliable, please note that individual situations can vary. Therefore, the information should be relied upon only when coordinated with individual professional advice. This material contains the current opinions of the author but not necessarily those of Guardian or its subsidiaries, and such opinions are subject to change without notice.

This material has not been endorsed by Guardian, its subsidiaries, agents, or employees. No representation or warranty, either express or implied, is provided in relation to the accuracy, completeness, or reliability of the information contained herein. In addition, the content does not necessarily represent the opinions of Guardian, its subsidiaries, agents, or employees.

Registered Representative and Financial Advisor of Park Avenue Securities LLC (PAS). OSJ: 200 Broadhollow Road, Suite 405, Melville, NY 11747, 631-589-5400. Securities products and advisory services offered through PAS, member FINRA, SIPC. Financial Representative of The Guardian Life Insurance Company of America®

(Guardian), New York, NY. PAS is a wholly owned subsidiary of Guardian. Northeast Private Client Group is not an affiliate or subsidiary of PAS or Guardian. CA Insurance License #0B36048, AR Insurance License #741545. 2022-143340

CPSIA information can be obtained
at www.ICGtesting.com
Printed in the USA
BVHW031332050323
659714BV00004B/13/J

9 781955 884259